AF834351

Basel III: Are We Done Now?

Institute for Law and Finance Series

Edited by
Theodor Baums
Andreas Cahn

Volume 21

Basel III: Are We Done Now?

Edited by
Andreas Dombret
Patrick S. Kenadjian

DE GRUYTER

ISBN 978-3-11-061973-7
e-ISBN (PDF) 978-3-11-062149-5
e-ISBN (EPUB) 978-3-11-061999-7

Library of Congress Control Number: 2018954005

Bibliografische Information der Deutschen Nationalbibliothek
Die Deutsche Nationalbibliothek verzeichnet diese Publikation in der Deutschen Nationalbibliografie; detaillierte bibliografische Daten sind im Internet über http://dnb.d-nb.de abrufbar.

© 2019 Walter de Gruyter GmbH, Berlin/Boston
Typesetting: Integra Software Services Pvt. Ltd.
Printing and binding:CPI books GmbH, Leck
Cover image: Medioimages/Photodisc

www.degruyter.com

Introduction

The first Duke of Wellington famously said of the Battle of Waterloo that it was "a near run thing." The same could be said of the last round of negotiations on the Basel III accords. Originally scheduled for December 2015, agreement was finally reached in December 2017, and not a moment too soon, both from a technical and a macro point of view. Technically, the participants were using 2015 data and, if negotiations had run beyond year end 2017 the pressure to start over with more up-to-date numbers would likely have led to further delay. From a macro point of view, this delay would have occurred at a point in time when the pendulum, which after the financial crisis had swung very much in the direction of regulatory reform, was perceptibly starting to swing back in the other direction. Such swings are natural and occur after every crisis, but in this case the political back drop, including a new administration in the United States committed to a deregulatory agenda and a persistent lack of vigorous growth in Europe, which some blamed on excessive regulation, led to fears that the deregulatory forces would accelerate before the work undertaken by the Financial Stability Board ("FSB") and the Basel Committee on Bank Supervision at the behest of the G20 would be completed.

So it was in a sense "now or never" in December 2017 when agreement was finally reached. To celebrate that milestone and to examine what exactly had and had not been agreed, on 29 January 2018, the Institute for Law and Finance at the Goethe University, Frankfurt am Main hosted a daylong conference entitled "Basel II: Are We Done Now?" at which we were honored to gather many of the participants in that regulatory marathon, together with distinguished academics and representatives of the private sector for a day of reflection looking both backward and forward.

The papers included in this volume are the results of that reflection. They show a general consensus that the agreement was very much a compromise, but on balance a good one, and far preferable to no deal, which would have risked breaking faith with the commitments entered into at the time the G20 was created, that we would strive to solve our problems together and not separately. Also, as many of the participants noted, reaching agreement on capital standards was essential to being able to turn the page from active new regulation to a reflection on what had been accomplished, what was good, and where we might have gone too far. It was essential from a public policy point of view to enable the Chair of the FSB to recommend in March of this year to the G20 that the time had come for "pivoting focus from new policy development toward evaluating policies that have been implemented," something which many participants referred to as a

https://doi.org/10.1515/9783110621495-201

"regulatory pause." However, there is to be no rest for the weary since many of the participants in the negotiations to reach an accord are the same people who will have to ensure that the agreed upon standards, which do not have the force of law, are implemented in a uniform manner across the various jurisdictions, and prior experience with FSB standards has shown how crucial uniform implementation is.

For the financial institutions to whom the standards will apply, the accord means a degree of certainty as to the extent of regulation that has been sorely lacking during the last years. With this comes more certainty for planning and developing business plans appropriate to their new environment and the prospect of an end to the uncertainty discount in their valuation in the market.

The day's deliberations also highlighted a number of areas even regarding bank capital, such as the risk weighting of sovereign debt, where additional work needs to be done, as well as a degree of regret over some roads not taken, but overall the view was that we have taken a great step forward and that while Basel III may not be remembered as a world historic event comparable to Waterloo; it had been a battle worth fighting and that the participants could be proud of the results achieved.

Andreas Dombret
Patrick Kenadjian

Frankfurt am Main, April 2018

Contents

VII: **Conclusion**

The Authors

Claudio Borio
Head of the Monetary and Economic Department, Bank for International Settlements, Basel, Switzerland

Claudio Borio was appointed Head of the Monetary and Economic Department on November 18 2013.

At the BIS since 1987, Borio has held various positions in the Monetary and Economic Department (MED), including Deputy Head of MED and Director of Research and Statistics as well as Head of Secretariat for the Committee on the Global Financial System and the Gold and Foreign Exchange Committee (now the Markets Committee). From 1985 to 1987, he was an economist at the OECD, working in the country studies branch of the Economics and Statistics Department. Prior to that, he was Lecturer and Research Fellow at Brasenose College, Oxford University. He holds a DPhil and an MPhil in Economics and a BA in Politics, Philosophy and Economics from the same university. Claudio is author of numerous publications in the fields of monetary policy, banking, finance and issues related to financial stability.

William Coen
Secretary General, Basel Committee on Banking Supervision, Bank for International Settlements, Basel, Switzerland

As Secretary General of the Basel Committee on Banking Supervision, Bill Coen directs its work and manages its Secretariat. The Basel Committee is the international group of central bankers and banking supervisors responsible for setting global banking standards.

Bill was appointed as Secretary General in 2014. He currently serves as chairman of the Basel Committee's Policy Development Group and has also chaired the Committee's Task Force on Corporate Governance and the Coherence and Calibration Task Force. Prior to his appointment as Secretary General, Bill served as Deputy Secretary General. Appointed to that role in 2007, he managed the daily activities and workstreams of the Basel Committee and its Secretariat. His specific responsibilities as Deputy Secretary General focused on the Basel Committee's response to the financial crisis, including the coordination of the Committee's various Basel III policy initiatives.

Bill joined the Basel Committee's Secretariat in 1999 from the Board of Governors of the Federal Reserve System in Washington D.C. During his career at the Federal Reserve, he worked in areas related to banking policy, supervision and licensing. Before joining the Federal Reserve, he was a bank examiner for the U.S. Office of the Comptroller of the Currency. Bill began his career as a credit officer

https://doi.org/10.1515/9783110621495-202

of a New York City-based bank, where he served as an Assistant Vice President responsible for consumer credit and retail mortgage lending.

Bill is a native of New York City and received his Master of Business Administration degree from Fordham University (1991) and Bachelor of Science degree from Manhattan College (1984).

Andreas Dombret
Member, Executive Board, Deutsche Bundesbank (May 2010-May 2018)
Member, Board of Directors, Bank for International Settlements, Basel
Andreas Dombret was born in the United States to German parents. He studied business management at the Westfälische Wilhelms University in Münster and earned his PhD at the Friedrich-Alexander University in Erlangen-Nuremberg.

From 1987 to 1991, he worked at Deutsche Bank's Head Office in Frankfurt, from 1992 to 2002 at JP Morgan in Frankfurt and London, from 2002 to 2005 as the Co-Head of Rothschild Germany located in Frankfurt and London, before serving Bank of America as Vice Chairman for Europe and Head for Germany, Austria and Switzerland between 2005 and 2009. He was awarded an honorary professorship from the European Business School in Oestrich-Winkel in 2009.

From May 2010 to May 2018, he has been a member of the Executive Board of the Deutsche Bundesbank with responsibility for Financial Stability, Statistics, Markets, Banking and Financial Supervision, Economic Education, Risk Controlling and the Bundesbank's Representative Offices abroad. He was also responsible for the IMF (Deputy of the Bundesbank), Financial Stability Commission (Member), Supervisory Board of the SSM (Member), Basel Committee on Banking Supervision (BCBS) (Member) and is still a member of the Board of Directors at the Bank for International Settlements, Basel.

Douglas J. Elliott
Partner, Oliver Wyman
He has written and spoken extensively on the impact of recent political developments on financial institutions, including writing "Financial Institutions in an Age of Populism" and "Implications of the Trump Administration for Financial Regulation." In 2016, Douglas was the lead author of a 150-page study analyzing the impacts of the Basel reforms, building on a similar paper from several years earlier for the IMF.

Prior to joining the firm, he was a Fellow in Economic Studies at The Brookings Institution, the world's leading think tank. At Brookings, he wrote and spoke extensively on financial regulation and its international coordination. He has been a Visiting Scholar at the International Monetary Fund, as well as a consultant for the IMF, the World Bank and the Asian Development Bank. He frequently appears on panels or as a speaker for the Basel Committee, FSB, Fed, IMF, World Bank, Bank of England, ECB, ESRB, Bundesbank, European Commission, JFSA, Asian Development Bank, U.S. Treasury, OCC, and other official bodies, as well as at trade group and industry functions.

Prior to Brookings, he was a financial institutions' investment banker for two decades, principally at J.P. Morgan. He worked across the range of financial institutions' clients, including banks, insurers and asset managers. He was primarily an M&A investment banker, but also worked as an equities analyst and in capital markets.

He has testified multiple times before both houses of Congress and participated in numerous speaking engagements, as well as appearing widely in the major media outlets. *The New York Times* has described his analyses as "refreshingly understandable" and "without a hint of dogma or advocacy."

Elliott graduated from Harvard College magna cum laude with an A.B. in Sociology in 1981. In 1984, he graduated from Duke University with an MA in Computer Science.

Andrea Enria
Chairperson of the EBA

Andrea Enria took office as the first Chairman of the European Banking Authority on March 1 2011. Before that date, he was the Head of the Regulation and Supervisory Policy Department at the Bank of Italy. He previously served as Secretary General of CEBS, dealing with technical aspects of EU banking legislation, supervisory convergence and cooperation within the EU. In the past, he also held the position of Head of Financial Supervision Division at the European Central Bank. Before joining the ECB, he worked for several years in the Research Department and in the Supervisory Department of the Bank of Italy. Enria has a BA in Economics from Bocconi University and a M. Phil. in Economics from Cambridge University.

Michael S. Gibson
Director, Division of Supervision and Regulation, Board of Governors of the Federal Reserve System

Michael S. Gibson is director of the Division of Supervision and Regulation at the Federal Reserve Board. As division director, he oversees the Federal Reserve's development of bank regulatory policy and its supervision of banking organizations. He works closely with officials from other U.S. and international government agencies on bank oversight issues.

He formerly served as deputy director in the Division of Research and Statistics at the Board of Governors of the Federal Reserve System, where he was responsible for overseeing the division's financial functions. He has worked on research and policy issues related to financial stability, financial markets and derivatives. He has authored articles on value at risk, stress testing and credit derivatives. He served on the faculty of the University of Chicago Graduate School of Business for 2 years and as a visiting lecturer at Princeton University. He has a PhD in economics from the Massachusetts Institute of Technology and a BA in economics from Stanford University.

Charles Goodhart

Emeritus Professor at the London School of Economics

Charles Goodhart, CBE, FBA is Emeritus Professor of Banking and Finance with the Financial Markets Group at the London School of Economics, having previously been its Deputy Director from 1987–2005. Until his retirement in 2002, he had been the Norman Sosnow Professor of Banking and Finance at LSE since 1985. Before then, he had worked at the Bank of England for 17 years as a monetary adviser, becoming a Chief Adviser in 1980. In 1997, he was appointed one of the outside independent members of the Bank of England's new Monetary Policy Committee until May 2000. Earlier he had taught at Cambridge and LSE. Besides numerous articles, he has written a couple of books on monetary history; a graduate monetary textbook, *Money, Information and Uncertainty* (2nd Ed. 1989); two collections of papers on monetary policy, *Monetary Theory and Practice* (1984) and *The Central Bank and The Financial System* (1995); and a number of books and articles on Financial Stability, on which subject he was Adviser to the Governor of the Bank of England from 2002–2004, and numerous other studies relating to financial markets and to monetary policy and history. His latest books include *The Basel Committee on Banking Supervision: A History of the Early Years, 1974–1997*, (2011), *and The Regulatory Response to the Financial Crisis,* (2009).

Stuart Graham

Partner, Banks Strategy, Autonomous Research

Prior to founding Autonomous in 2009, Stuart was the head of European banks equity research at Merrill Lynch. Before joining Merrill Lynch in 2002, Stuart worked at JPMorgan and HSBC (both in banks equity research). He began his career at the Bank of England in 1988 in the banking supervision department. Stuart holds an MA in modern history from Cambridge University.

Paul Hilbers

Director Financial Stability at the Netherlands Bank

Paul was appointed Director of Financial Stability at the Netherlands Bank (DNB) in May 2015. He is a member of the Financial Stability Board's Standing Committee on Assessment of Vulnerabilities and alternate member of the BIS Committee on the Global Financial System. In addition, he is the Secretary of the Dutch Financial Stability Committee, a member of the Council of the Netspar Foundation and an external member of the Audit Committee of the Ministry of Foreign Affairs.

Before taking up his current position, Paul was Director of Supervision Policy at DNB. He has been a member of the Basel Committee and (co-)chair of the Task Forces on Impact & Accountability of Banking Supervision and Sovereign Exposures. Earlier in his career, he worked at the International Monetary Fund (IMF) in Washington for over 15 years. During that period, he served as Manager in the IMF's Monetary and Capital Markets Department and Division Chief and Mission Chief in the European Department.

Paul Hilbers was appointed part-time professor at Nyenrode Business Universiteit (NBU) in 2010. His field is Financial Sector Supervision and his chair is part of the Supervision Academy at NBU. Paul specializes in research that contributes to the further development of supervision and regulation of the financial sector.

Paul studied Mathematics at the University of Utrecht (BA) and Econometrics at the Free University in Amsterdam (MA), where he also obtained his PhD in International Economics. He has published extensively on monetary, fiscal and financial sector issues.

Dr. Levin Holle
Director General, Financial Markets Policy Department, Federal Ministry of Finance, Berlin, Germany
Levin Holle is the Head of the Financial Markets Policy Department of Germany's Federal Ministry of Finance. His responsibilities include the formulation of policies and strategies with respect to federal credit institutions, federal debt management, financial markets as well as anti-money laundering and international financial markets policy. He is also responsible for the supervision of the Federal Financial Supervisory Authority and the Financial Market Stabilisation Authority. Additionally, he is supervisory board member of the Deutsche Bahn AG since 2018.

Prior to joining the German Finance Ministry, he worked for 15 years at the management consultancy Boston Consulting Group, his last position being Senior Partner and Managing Director of the Berlin office. In 1996, he earned his PhD from the University of Göttingen.

Stefan Ingves
Governor of the Riksbank and Chairman of the Executive Board, Sveriges Riksbank
Stefan Ingves is Governor of the Riksbank and Chairman of the Executive Board. Ingves holds a PhD in Economics from Stockholm School of Economics.

Ingves has previously been Director of the Monetary and Financial Systems Department at the IMF, Deputy Governor of the Riksbank and Director General of the Swedish Bank Support Authority. Prior to that he was Under-Secretary and Head of the Financial Markets Department at the Ministry of Finance.

International assignments include Chairman of the Basel Committee, Chairman of the BIS Banking and Risk Committee and Member of Board of Directors of the BIS, Member of the General Council of the ECB, Member of the General Board of the European Systemic Risk Board (ESRB) and Governor for Sweden of the IMF.

Patrick Kenadjian
Senior Counsel, Davis Polk & Wardwell LLP
Patrick is currently an Adjunct Professor at the Goethe University in Frankfurt am Main, Germany, where he teaches courses on the financial crisis and financial reform and mergers and acquisitions at the Institute for Law and Finance.

Patrick has chaired conferences at the Goethe University in Frankfurt on bank culture and ethics, the EU's Capital Markets Initiative, "too big to fail," the EU's Bank Recovery and Resolution Directive and the EU's Collective Action Clause initiative and sovereign debt restructuring. He speaks frequently on topics related to financial reform, including "too big to fail," the architecture of financial supervision and the new regulatory environment in the United States and the EU. He has acted as Program Director for the Salzburg Global Seminar's Finance in a Changing World Series in 2013 and 2014 and is currently a member of its Advisory Committee.

Patrick is also Senior Counsel at Davis Polk & Wardwell London LLP. He was a partner of the firm from 1984 to 2010, during which time he opened the firm's Tokyo and Frankfurt offices in 1987 and 1991, respectively and spent over 25 years in its European and Asian offices. He speaks French, German and Italian.

He has been listed as a leading lawyer in several industry publications, including *Chambers Global: The World's Leading Lawyers for Business and Legal Media Group's Expert Guide to the World's Leading Banking Lawyers, Expert Guide to the World's Leading Capital Markets Lawyers and Expert Guide to the World's Leading Lawyers Best of the Best."*

Sabine Lautenschläger
Member of the Executive Board & Vice-Chair of the Supervisory Board of the European Central Bank
Sabine Lautenschläger was born in Stuttgart in 1964. She studied law in Bonn. After passing the second state examination in law, she joined the Bundesaufsichtsamt für das Kreditwesen (BAKred – Federal Banking Supervisory Office),

which later became the Bundesanstalt für Finanzdienstleistungsaufsicht (BaFin – Federal Financial Supervisory Authority). In the course of her career at BAKred/BaFin, she held several management positions before being appointed BaFin's Chief Executive Director of Banking Supervision in 2008. Later, in 2011, she additionally was Member of the Management Board and Board of Supervisors of the European Banking Authority (EBA) in London.

In 2011, Sabine Lautenschläger moved to the Deutsche Bundesbank, serving as Vice-President until January 2014 when she was appointed to the Executive Board of the European Central Bank. As Member of the Executive Board, she is also Member of the Governing Council, which is responsible for the Monetary Policy in the Euro Area. Since her appointment as Vice-Chair of the Supervisory Board of the Single Supervisory Mechanism (SSM) in February 2014, she has also been in charge of ECB Banking Supervision. She represents ECB Banking Supervision in the Basel Committee on Banking Supervision and in the Financial Stability Board Plenary.

Laurie Mayers
Associate Managing Director, Moody's Investors Service

Laurie Mayers is an Associate Managing Director in the Financial Institutions Group at Moody's Investors Service based in London.

She has responsibility for the portfolio of banks and non-bank financial institutions, which Moody's rates in the United Kingdom and Ireland as well as for the global investment banks in Europe and the United States.

Laurie is also a key contributor to Moody's engagement with investors on regulatory issues such as Basel III, the implementation of the BRRD, UK ring-fencing and the implications of Brexit.

Prior to joining Moody's in 2012, Laurie worked for the UK Financial Services Authority, managing the team responsible for the co-ordination of firm-wide stress testing exercises on the large UK banks as well as for Pillar II capital assessments as part of the Supervisory Review and Evaluation Process (SREP). Her experience prior to the FSA included global and divisional risk and regulatory roles within investment banking division and group risk functions at institutions including RBS/NatWest, ING and Morgan Stanley. Originally from New York, Laurie commenced her banking career at Chase Manhattan Bank where she completed the in-house credit training programme before becoming a lending officer in the Commodity Finance division. She holds a BA in Political Economy from Williams College and a Masters in International Affairs with a specialization in International Economics from Columbia University.

Martin Merlin
Director, Regulation and Prudential Supervision of Financial Institutions Directorate General for Financial Stability, Financial Services and Capital Markets Union European Commission, Brussels
He started his career at the French Treasury in the Department of International Monetary and Financial Affairs.

In 1997, he joined the Commission and since then has worked consistently across the various domains of Financial Services including positions in the Commissioner's Cabinet, as policy Assistant to the Director General, as Head of Unit coordinating Financial Services Policy and as Director of Financial Markets until his current position responsible for banking and insurance regulation.

He represents the Commission at the Basel Committee and on the Board of Supervisors at both EBA & EIOPA.

Masters Degree – Political science
Masters Degree – Philosophy

Sandie O'Connor
Managing Director, Chief Regulatory Affairs Officer, JPMorgan Chase & Co.
Sandie O'Connor is the Chief Regulatory Affairs Officer for JPMorgan Chase & Co. She also serves on firmwide governance committees and chairs the JPMorgan Chase Foundation Investment Committee.

As Chief Regulatory Affairs Officer, O'Connor sets the firm's comprehensive regulatory strategy and leads engagement with G-20 international standard setters, regulators and policy-makers regarding evolving regulation and legislation. She provides meaningful perspective on the impact of evolving financial stability regulation on clients, business activities and economic growth using quantitative analysis and a deep understanding of capital flows, balance sheets and market liquidity. She is also a thought leader on emerging areas of policy, including cybersecurity, fintech, data use and privacy, creating focus, building common understanding and driving for collaborative solutions.

O'Connor joined J.P. Morgan in 1988 and has held several key executive positions. Most recently, she was Treasurer of JPMorgan Chase, where she managed the firm's capital, balance sheet, liquidity and funding strategy and positions, as well as the firm's rating agency relationships and corporate insurance activities.

O'Connor serves on the boards of several industry trade associations, including the Securities Industry and Financial Markets Association and as Chair of the Global Financial Markets Association. She also serves as the chair of the Federal Reserve's Alternative Reference Rates Committee, member of the Treasury Markets

Practitioners Group, member of the Office of Financial Research Advisory Committee and Chair of an Advisory Committee of the Salzburg Global Seminar.

In addition to her work, O'Connor also serves as Vice Chair of the Board of Directors of the YMCA of Greater New York and Chair of its Development Committee.

Christian Ossig
Chief Executive of the Association of German Banks
Christian Ossig is Chief Executive of the Association of German Banks and a former investment banker.

He is a member of the Executive Committee of the European Banking Federation (EBF), a Supervisory Board member of the German Federal Financial Supervisory Authority (BaFin) and the German Accounting Standards Board (DRSC). He heads the German private banks' deposit insurance scheme and, in this role, serves on the supervisory boards of several commercial banks.

Christian started his career in investment banking at JPMorgan in London and worked as a financial institutions expert at NM Rothschild. He then became Managing Director and Member of the Management Board at Bank of America in Frankfurt and The Royal Bank of Scotland. Before joining the Association of German Banks, he worked at the Institute of International Finance (IIF) in Washington, D.C. Christian studied for his undergraduate degree in business and international economics at the European Partnership of Business Schools in Germany and France, and for his Master's degree and PhD at the College of Europe in Belgium and Cambridge University in the United Kingdom.

Isabel Schnabel
Professor of Financial Economics, Member of the German Council of Economic Experts
Isabel Schnabel has been a Professor of Financial Economics at the University of Bonn since 2015. In 2014, she became a Member of the German Council of Economic Experts (Sachverständigenrat zur Begutachtung der gesamtwirtschaftlichen Entwicklung), an independent advisory body of the German government. She is Research Fellow at the Centre for Economic Policy Research (CEPR) in London and at the CESifo in Munich, and Research Affiliate at the Max Planck Institute for Research on Collective Goods in Bonn. Moreover, Isabel Schnabel is a member of the Administrative and Advisory Councils of the German Federal Financial Supervisory Authority (BaFin) and of the Advisory Scientific Committee (ASC) of the European Systemic Risk Board (ESRB). Her research focuses on financial stability, banking regulation, international capital flows and economic history.

Shunsuke Shirakawa
Vice Commissioner for International Affairs, Financial Services Agency, Government of Japan

Shunsuke Shirakawa is Vice Commissioner for International Affairs at Japan's Financial Services Agency (JFSA). He represents the agency at the Standing Committee on Supervisory and Regulatory Cooperation (SRC) and the Resolution Steering Group (ReSG) of the Financial Stability Board (FSB) as well as the Basel Committee on Banking Supervision (BCBS). He is also contributing to regional cooperation among bank supervisors as Vice Chair of the EMEAP Working Group on Banking Supervision.

Shirakawa joined the Ministry of Finance of Japan in 1986, and has held various positions at the JFSA, including Deputy-Director General of the Planning and Coordination Bureau (Policy Coordination); Director of the Evaluation Division, Inspection Bureau; Director of the Insurance Business Division, Supervisory Bureau; Director of the Office of International Affairs; and Private Secretary to Minister for Financial Services.

He holds an LLB degree from the University of Tokyo (1986) and a MPA degree from the Columbia University (1990).

I: Basel III

Stefan Ingves, Chairman, Basel Committee on Banking Supervision

Basel III: Are we done now?

Introduction

The title of this conference is “Basel III: Are we done now?” Let me answer this question at the outset: yes, we are done, but that doesn’t mean the work has ended. In some respects, it’s only just the beginning. While finalising Basel III was an important milestone, work remains to (i) implement Basel III nationally in a full, timely and consistent manner; (ii) evaluate its effectiveness in reducing the excessive variability of risk-weighted assets (RWAs); and (iii) continue to monitor and assess emerging risks. My remarks this morning will focus on these three topics.

Basel III: from 2010 to 2017

But let me start with a brief review of the Basel III framework, which has been 10 years in the making.

As you know, the Basel III framework is a central element of the Basel Committee’s response to the global financial crisis. The initial phase of Basel III reforms, published in 2010 (BCBS 2010[a]), focused on addressing some of the main shortcomings of the pre-crisis regulatory framework, including:

- Improving the quality of bank regulatory capital by placing a greater focus on going-concern loss-absorbing capital in the form of Common Equity Tier 1 (CET1) capital
- Increasing capital requirements to ensure that banks can withstand losses in times of stress
- Enhancing risk capture by revising areas of the risk-weighted capital framework that proved to be acutely miscalibrated, including the global standards for market risk, counterparty credit risk and securitisation
- Adding macroprudential elements to the regulatory framework, by: (i) introducing capital buffers that are built-up in good times and can be drawn down in times of stress to limit procyclicality; (ii) establishing a large exposures regime that mitigates systemic risks arising from interlinkages across financial institutions and concentrated exposures; and (iii) putting in place a capital buffer to address the externalities created by systemically important banks

https://doi.org/10.1515/9783110621495-001

- Specifying a minimum leverage ratio requirement to constrain excess leverage in the banking system and complement the risk-weighted capital requirements
- Introducing an international framework for mitigating excessive liquidity risk and maturity transformation, through the Liquidity Coverage Ratio and Net Stable Funding Ratio

These reforms have demonstrably helped to strengthen the global banking system. Since 2011, the Tier 1 leverage ratio of major internationally active banks has increased by over 65% (from 3.5% to 5.8%), while their CET1 risk-weighted ratio has increased by over 70% (from 7.2% to 12.3%). The bulk of this change was achieved by an increase in banks' CET1 capital resources (from €2.1 trillion to €3.7 trillion). There has also been a corresponding reinforcement of banks' liquidity: holdings of liquid assets have increased by 30% (from €9.2 trillion to €11.6 trillion).

There are also clear social benefits from these reforms. During the global financial crisis, the weaknesses in the banking sector were transmitted to the rest of the financial system and the real economy, resulting in substantial costs. Ten years after the start of the crisis, the global economy is still recovering from its effects. These costs include much higher public debt, increased unemployment and substantial output losses. To give just one example, a recent study estimates that the cumulative output loss resulting from financial crises is in the order of 100% of GDP in net present value terms.[1] This output loss would probably have been much larger without the massive public sector interventions. The increase in banks' capital and liquidity resources will help mitigate both the probability and impact of future banking crises.

But a major faultline remained in the regulatory framework, namely, the way in which RWAs were calculated. At the peak of the global financial crisis, a wide range of stakeholders lost faith in banks' internally modelled risk-weighted capital ratios. The complexity and opacity of internal models, the degree of discretion provided to banks in modelling risk parameters and the use of national discretions all contributed to an excessive degree of RWA variation. A growing number of studies by authorities, academics and the private sector pointed to a worryingly large variation in banks' estimated RWAs (BCBS [2013a, b]). For example, one study found that banks' reported capital ratios could vary by 50% for the same hypothetical portfolio.[2] The loss in the public's confidence in banks'

1 Fender and Lewrick (2016).
2 BCBS (2013a).

reported capital ratios clearly highlighted the need for tighter limits to the way in which RWAs are calculated and greater transparency.

The recently finalised Basel III reforms seek to restore the credibility of RWA calculations, and as a result the public's confidence in the banking system, by:

- Enhancing the robustness and risk sensitivity of the standardised approaches for credit risk and operational risk, which will make banks' capital ratios more comparable
- Constraining the use of internally modelled approaches, including removing the use of the most advanced modelled approaches for certain credit risk asset classes and for calculating operational risk
- Complementing the risk-weighted capital ratio with a finalised leverage ratio and a revised and robust output floor

Collectively, the set of Basel III reforms addresses a number of shortcomings in the pre-crisis regulatory framework and provides a foundation for a resilient banking system that will help mitigate the impact of future banking crises and the build-up of systemic vulnerabilities. The post-crisis framework will also help the banking system support the real economy and contribute to economic growth.

Full, timely and consistent implementation: more than just words

But are these reforms enough, or does more need to be done? The answer depends in part on the extent to which the reforms are implemented in a full, timely and consistent manner across jurisdictions. To borrow the words of Goethe (1829): "willing is not enough, we must do."

The Basel Committee's standards are global *minimum* standards. The Committee has no supranational authority, its decisions carry no legal force and it cannot impose fines or sanctions. Rather, once the Committee agrees on a standard, its member jurisdictions are responsible for converting this standard into law or regulation. So internationally agreed standards that are not properly implemented will ultimately have no impact in practice. It is therefore imperative that the Basel standards are effectively implemented by all the Committee's jurisdictions.

To this end, the Committee's flagship Regulatory Consistency Assessment Programme (RCAP) monitors the timely adoption of Basel standards across jurisdictions and reviews whether standards are completely and consistently adopted by member jurisdictions. They also highlight any deviations from the Basel framework. As a result of the RCAPs, over 1,200 deviations were identified as part of the peer reviews focusing on the initial Basel III capital reforms. Two-thirds of Basel Committee members have risk-weighted capital rules that are considered compliant or largely compliant with the Basel capital standards.

Looking forward, the RCAP will continue to play a key role in ensuring that the recently finalised Basel III reforms are implemented as agreed by the Committee. But let me stress three points.

First, in developing its standards, the Committee actively seeks the views of all stakeholders: public and private. For example, in finalising Basel III, the Committee consulted extensively with academics, analysts, banks, finance ministries, parliamentarians, market participants and trade associations as well as the general public. These views were duly considered by the Committee in finalising its standards. So there are plenty of opportunities for all stakeholders to express their views before the standards are finalised. The focus then should be on full, timely and consistent implementation.

Second, in endorsing the finalised Basel III reforms, the Group of Governors and Heads of Supervision (GHOS) has unanimously reaffirmed that they expect full, timely and consistent implementation "of all elements" of the Basel III package (BCBS [2017a]). So I take comfort that all of the Committee's members keep this aim in the forefront of their minds during the implementation phase.

Third, the move to national implementation should not be read as an invitation to reopen policy issues and debates at a domestic level. While the varying legislative and procedural arrangements used to implement Basel standards across the Committee's membership must be fully respected, it is concerning to see ongoing lobbying efforts by some banks and other stakeholders to undo or dilute aspects of the agreed Basel standards in some jurisdictions. The unsound expedient of adopting standards that fall below the Basel Committee's minimums can only lead to regulatory fragmentation, and in a bad scenario a potential race to the bottom.

Just getting up close, as we like to say in Sweden, isn't enough to shoot the hare.

Reducing excessive RWA variability: mission accomplished?

Assuming that the Basel reforms are properly implemented, will they reduce excessive RWA variability and restore the credibility of the risk-weighted capital framework? While I am confident that the Basel III reforms are an important step in that direction, the honest answer is that only time will tell.

To that end, the Committee has initiated a rigorous evaluation of its post-crisis reforms, including those that relate to reducing excessive RWA variability. As the reforms will only start to be implemented from 2022 onwards, this exercise will take several years. But I believe that the Committee should remain open to the possibility of considering whether additional measures, or revisions to existing measures, are warranted to reduce excessive RWA variability.

In a similar vein, the Committee is also further evaluating the interactions and coherence of its post-crisis reforms. The findings will provide an important input for future deliberations by the Committee about the robustness and effectiveness of its post-crisis framework.

I will not prejudge the outcomes of these evaluations, but let me make three observations. First, the purpose of these evaluations is not to reopen already agreed standards. Second, the Basel Committee is a member-led and consensus-based body. Accordingly, the Basel III reforms are a compromise that reflects the different views of its members. Third, as the Basel reforms are minimum standards, jurisdictions are welcome to apply more conservative requirements should they wish to do so. This could include faster transitional arrangements and/or more conservative steady-state requirements.

Enhancing financial stability: an ongoing journey

If the Basel reforms do reduce excessive RWA variability, is the job then done? Probably far from it. Banking crises are inevitable. So, while the Basel standards cannot prevent all future crises, they can seek to mitigate their likelihood and impact. This, in turn, requires the Basel Committee to remain vigilant for emerging conjunctural and structural risks. It also needs to monitor how banks are responding to its post-crisis reforms. All this highlights the importance of supervision as a complementary tool to regulation. Let me say a few remarks about both these issues.

Emerging risks

An example of a topical risk of direct relevance for the Basel Committee is cyber risk. The banking system is increasingly reliant on information technology, which exposes it to a growing and evolving set of operational risks. Banks with operationally resilient systems, staff, processes and technology can better adapt to evolving shocks and maintain the provision of critical financial services. The Committee is reviewing its existing cyber-risk measures and will consider whether additional measures are needed to enhance banks' operational resilience.

Behavioural responses to post-crisis reforms

With the Committee's post-crisis reforms now finalised, and with only minor technical issues remaining, the Basel Committee will carefully monitor banks' responses to its reforms. It will continuously assess banks' behavioural responses, and the potential emergence of any optimisation or arbitrage techniques that may not meet the letter or spirit of the Basel standards. In this case, it will consider whether any measures are needed to address such issues.

Supervision

The Committee's response to the global financial crisis included much more than just regulation. It also encompassed a range of measures to support strong supervision. These include principles and guidance on corporate governance, risk data aggregation, the prudential treatment of assets, the treatment of weak banks and an updated set of core principles for effective banking supervision. The Committee will step up its efforts to promote improvements in banking supervision practices and principles.

Conclusion

In summary, the finalisation of Basel III in December 2017 represents an important milestone for the Basel Committee's response to the global financial crisis. The full set of Basel III reforms will help enhance the resilience of the banking system. But we cannot rest on our laurels. Whether it relates to the proper implementation of these reforms, their evaluation or the assessment of emerging risks, the Basel Committee will continue to exercise its mandate to strengthen the regulation, supervision and practices of banks worldwide. The agenda changes, but the purpose is constant – to safeguard and enhance financial stability.

References

Basel Committee on Banking Supervision, BCBS (2006): *Basel II: International convergence of capital measurement and capital standards: a revised framework - Comprehensive Version*, June.

— (2010a): *Basel III: A global regulatory framework for more resilient banks and banking systems*, December.

— (2010b): *An assessment of the long-term economic impact of stronger capital and liquidity requirements*, August.

— (2013a): "Analysis of risk-weighted assets for credit risk in the banking book", *Regulatory Consistency Assessment Programme (RCAP)*, July.

— (2013b): "Analysis of risk-weighted assets for market risk", *Regulatory Consistency Assessment Programme (RCAP)*, January and December.

— (2015): "Finalising post-crisis reforms: an update", BCBS report to G20 Leaders, November.

— (2016): "Literature review on integration of regulatory capital and liquidity instruments", *BCBS Working Papers*, no 30, March.

— (2017a): *Press release: Governors and Heads of Supervision finalise Basel III reforms*, 7 December.

— (2017b): *Basel III: finalising post-crisis reforms*, December.

— (2017c): *Basel III Monitoring Report*, December.

Fender, I and Lewrick, U (2016): "Adding it all up: The macroeconomic impact of Basel III and outstanding reform issues", *BIS Working Papers*, No 591, November.

Goethe, J (1829): Wilhelm Meister's Journeyman Years, or the Renunciants, Cotta'sche Buchandlung, Stuttgart.

Ingves, S (2014): "Implementing the regulatory reform agenda – the pitfall of myopia", November.

— (2015): "From the Vasa to the Basel framework: The dangers of instability", November.

— (2016a): "Reflections of a Basel Committee Chairman", November.

— (2016b): "Finalising Basel III: Coherence, calibration and complexity", December.

II: Basel III: A milestone achievement?

William Coen, Secretary General, Basel Committee on Banking Supervision

Finalising Basel III

As the substance of the finalised Basel III reforms has been well publicised, I thought it would be useful for me to discuss not only what is in Basel III but what is *still* in the framework. The first thing I would like to point out is the framework's risk sensitivity. It is well known that the Basel Committee agreed on an aggregate output floor[1] of 72.5%, which is lower than the 80% that was previously agreed as an element of the Basel II framework. In addition, the internal risk-based approach (IRB) remains a central part of the risk-based capital framework. Even though the Basel II framework and the use of internal models for regulatory capital purposes came into effect only from around 2009, some important lessons were learned from the crisis and, based on this experience, the Committee has brought the pendulum back to a credible place. I will return in a moment to the relative importance of risk sensitivity and the need to balance it with simplicity and comparability.

One aspect of the Committee's December 2017 regulatory reforms is easily overlooked but it is of significant impact and importance: I'm speaking of the standardised approach for credit risk. The new standardised approach is a tremendous improvement on the previous standard and it now represents a realistic alternative to the internally modelled approach. This is important, of course, to the world's largest banks because the standardised approach forms the basis for how the output floor is calculated. But it is of even greater significance to more than 100 countries around the world and their banks that use the Basel Committee standards, since the majority of banks use the standardised approach. Not every jurisdiction in the world needs to offer the option of using the IRB approach and not every bank in the world needs to use the IRB. We have narrowed the gap between IRB and the standardised approach and this is good from a competitive, level playing field perspective.

What else is in the finalised package of reforms? A firm commitment on the part of the Basel Committee and its governing body – the Group of Central Bank Governors and Heads of Supervision (GHOS) – to review, monitor and assess the impact of the reforms. This process has already started and it is imperative that it is informed by data, research and analysis. As a matter of good public

1 An output floor limits the benefit enjoyed by a bank that has received supervisory authorisation to use its internal models for regulatory capital purposes. With an output floor of 72.5%, a bank that is permitted to use its internal models to calculate its regulatory capital receives a benefit of 27.5% versus the standardised approach.

https://doi.org/10.1515/9783110621495-002

policymaking, the Basel Committee needs to assess what it has put in place over these past 10 years and to determine whether the results produced by the standards meet our original expectations (BCBS [2010]). I chair a group that reports to the Basel Committee – the Policy Development Group – that is carefully reviewing this topic. Bearing in mind the original aims of the standards, we are seeking to answer questions such as the following: Are those objectives being met? What are the incentives arising from the new rules? How are banks responding to the new rules? Are there already behavioural changes to be observed? Have there already been changes to business models, strategies and activities? What about regulatory arbitrage? Are the letter and the spirit of the rules being circumvented? If so, what should be our response? As I noted, any type of impact analysis must be data-driven and based on empirical analysis.

What's *not* in the Basel III package? Technically speaking, the treatment of sovereign exposures was not part of the package but, from my perspective, this is still an active and open issue. At the same time as we published the Basel III revisions, we also published a "discussion paper" on the treatment of sovereign exposures. The Basel Committee members did not arrive at a consensus on proposing alternative treatments to the existing treatment of sovereign exposures but there certainly was a clear recognition of the importance of this topic. The Committee agreed to publish its latest thinking on the topic with the expectation that feedback from interested stakeholders would help inform the Committee's longer-term thinking on this important issue.

Risk sensitivity

I would now like to return to the issue of risk sensitivity. While the completion of the Basel III reforms represented a landmark achievement, one element of the Committee's post-crisis reform agenda has yet to be fully finalised: the market risk framework. The global financial crisis exposed fault lines in the Basel II market risk framework. The framework's low capital requirement for market risk was far eclipsed by the market risk losses of many banks. As a stopgap response, the Committee introduced a set of revisions (the so-called Basel 2.5 framework). These sought to reduce the framework's cyclicality and increase overall capital. There was a particular focus on instruments exposed to credit risk (including securitisations), where the previous regime had been found especially lacking.

However, the Committee recognised at the time that Basel 2.5 did not fully address the framework's shortcomings. As a result, the Committee undertook a fundamental review of the trading book regime (BCBS [2012]). This sought to

address shortcomings in the regime's design as well as weaknesses in risk measurement under both the internal model-based and standardised approaches, including the following:
- The trading book/banking book boundary
- Incorporating the risk of market illiquidity
- Enhancing the robustness and risk sensitivity of the standardised approach
- Capitalising against tail risk

In short, the pre-crisis market risk framework was in need of major repair. The weaknesses exposed by the crisis were also a stark reminder of the shortcomings in banks' own risk management practices and the limitations of models in general.

Market risk

After several years of work that included multiple consultations and quantitative impact studies (QIS), the Committee published a revised standard for the market risk framework in January 2016 (BCBS [2016]). As part of finalising the Basel III framework (BCBS [2017]), ongoing challenges in implementing certain bank capital reforms were acknowledged by the GHOS. Accordingly, the GHOS endorsed the Committee's proposal to extend the implementation date of the revised market risk framework from January 1, 2019 to January 1, 2022 (for both the implementation and first regulatory reporting date for the revised framework).

Deferring its implementation will also align the framework's starting date with those of the Basel III revisions for credit risk and operational risk. It will give banks more time to develop the systems needed to apply it.

More recently, the Committee issued a consultation paper in March 2018 proposing changes to the revised market risk framework. These include revisions to the calibration of certain elements of the standardised approach, and to the assessment process that determines whether a bank's internal risk management models appropriately reflect the risks of individual trading desks (BCBS [2018b]).

So there have been many developments related to the market risk framework even after the publication of the revised standard in early 2016. Let me offer three reflections on what more needs to be done to finalise the market risk rules.

First, as I mentioned earlier, market risk is important. It was a major source of losses for banks during the global financial crisis. And episodes of market risk-related stress can often catalyse credit risk and liquidity risk concerns, and vice versa. Many of the activities captured in the trading book, such as market-making and capital-raising, help support the real economy. So it is important that the prudential regulatory framework for market risk is calibrated to ensure the safety and soundness of the banking system, and, subject to achieving this objective, that it mitigates any unintended impacts on socially useful market activities. This is why the Committee has repeatedly consulted on its revisions to the market risk framework over the past several years, and why it has been engaging closely with International Swaps and Derivatives Association (ISDA) and other external stakeholders on its finalisation.

Second, although market risk is significant for banks with large and complex trading portfolios, the revisions to the market risk framework may at times have suffered from an illusory quest for "perfect" risk sensitivity (Ingves [2015]), resulting in a disproportionate use of both the Committee's time and that of external stakeholders. Consider the following facts:

- In aggregate, market risk accounts for the smallest share of total capital requirements across the main risk categories. This is the case both for relatively large internationally active banks and for small ones. As at end-June 2017, it comprised less than 5% and 2.5% of total minimum required capital for such banks, respectively (Figures 1 and 2).
- This share has only become smaller over time. Since 31 December 2011, the share of market risk as a proportion of total minimum required capital has

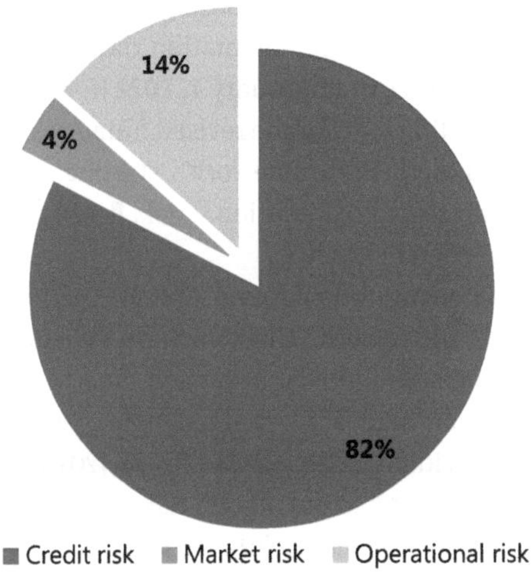

Figure 1: Share of capital requirements for Group 1 banks by risk category[(a)(b)]
Source: BCBS (2018a), p 31 and Secretariat calculations.
(a) As at end-June 2017. Sample consists of 106 internationally active banks with Tier 1 capital greater than €3 billion.
(b) Composition of banks' minimum required capital by risk category. Ignores any impact due to IRB provisioning shortfalls or the Basel I floor.

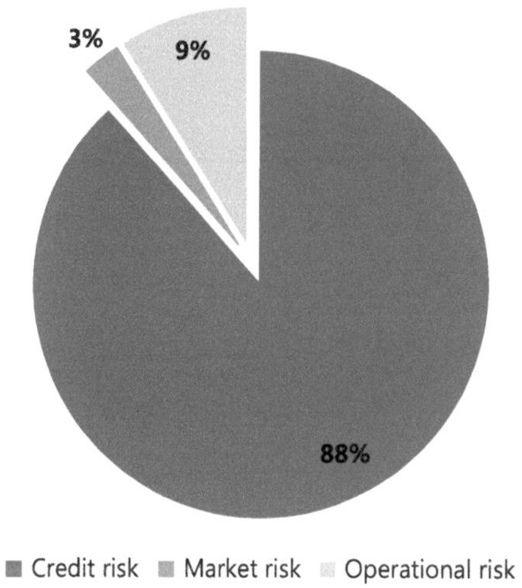

Figure 2: Share of capital requirements for Group 2 banks by risk category[(a)(b)]
Source: BCBS (2018a) p 31 and Secretariat calculations
(a) As at end-June 2017. Sample consists of 87 internationally active banks with Tier 1 capital less than €3 billion.
(b) Composition of banks' minimum required capital by risk category. Ignores any impact due to IRB provisioning shortfalls or the Basel I floor.

almost halved for larger banks, including global systemically important banks (Figure 3).[2]

- The overall capital impact of the revised market risk framework is relatively small for almost all banks. Based on an earlier analysis by the Committee prior to the finalisation of the revised market risk framework, the average change in market risk capital requirements resulting from the revised framework is about 5% of total capital requirements (Figure 5).[3] But there are a handful of "outlier" banks that would see a more significant increase or reduction of their market risk capital requirements.

---

2 The small contribution of market risk to capital requirements stands in stark contrast to the amount of resources devoted to the market risk framework. A simple, if crude, way of measuring the time and resources devoted to market risk is to calculate the ratio of the share of publications by the Committee since 1980 on different risk categories vis-à-vis the share of each risk category to total capital requirements. Suffice it to say, we have issued about six times as many publications as you would expect from just looking at the share of market risk as a percentage of total capital requirements. And this ratio increases to 10 times if the ratio is based on the number of references in Committee publications (Figure 4).

3 This does not reflect subsequent modifications included in the revised framework upon its finalisation, which led to a reduction in the average number.

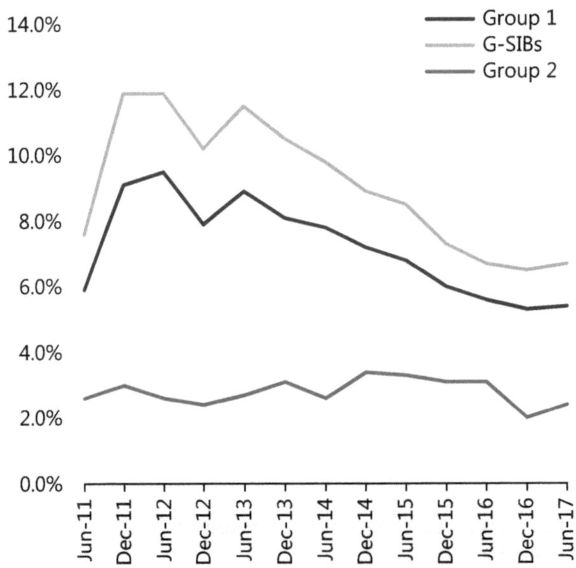

Figure 3: Share of market risk to total minimum required capital[a]
Source: BCBS (2018a), p 35.
(a) Sample of 36 Group 1 banks, 14 G-SIBs and 20 Group 2 banks.

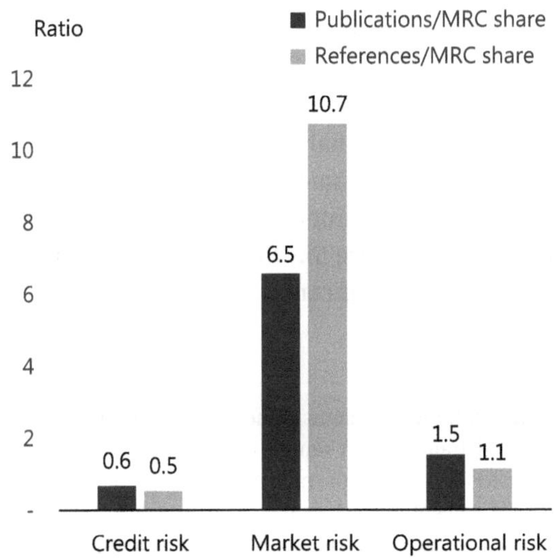

Figure 4: BCBS publications by risk category relative to share of capital requirements[a]
Source: BCBS and Secretariat calculations.
(a) Figure shows the ratio of total BCBS publications and references since 1980 related to major risk categories over the share of each risk category to minimum required capital.

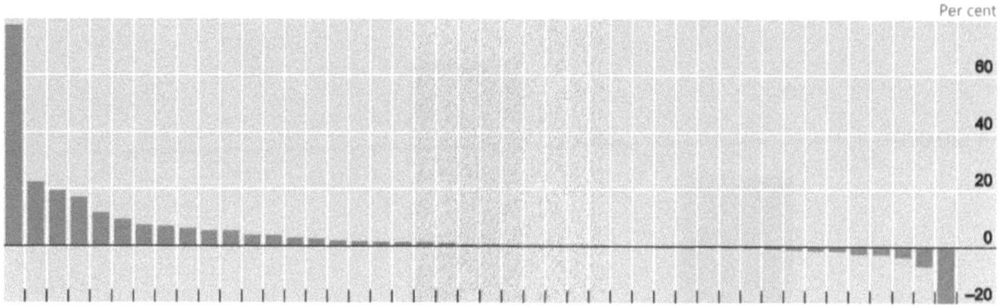

Figure 5: Change in total market risk capital requirements as a percentage of total Basel III minimum capital requirements as a result of revised market risk framework[(a)]
Source: BCBS (2015) p 3.
(a) As at end-December 2014, for a sample of 44 banks.

Simplicity, comparability and risk sensitivity: striking the right balance

Faced with these facts, an open question is whether the revised market risk framework has adequately balanced simplicity, comparability and risk sensitivity. In the run-up to our completion of the Basel framework revisions in December 2017, a common refrain was the need to maintain risk sensitivity. There was a concern – misguided in my view – that the imposition of an output floor and other measures under consideration by the Committee would impair the framework's risk sensitivity. The Committee has previously reaffirmed its support for a risk-weighted capital regime and its belief that it should remain at the core of the framework for banks, complemented by the leverage ratio and liquidity metrics. The Committee has also noted, however, that the pursuit of increased risk sensitivity has considerably increased the complexity of the capital adequacy framework in some areas – particularly the calculation methodology for risk-weighted assets (BCBS (2013b)).

I worry that it is often assumed that increased risk sensitivity is a priority of the banking industry and the pursuit of simplicity and comparability are the goals of supervisors. However, the financial crisis demonstrated quite clearly that, if the risk-weighted regime is too opaque or the reported results it produces are not credible (eg due to excessive variability among banks), market participants will simply stop using risk-weighted ratios to assess the health of banks Figure 6. Put another way, the more complex the risk-weighted regime becomes, the more the importance of other measures such as the leverage ratio will grow as an indicator of bank strength.

It seems, therefore, that it is in the interests of the banking industry itself to ensure that the regulatory regime is robust throughout the cycle. Further, that it

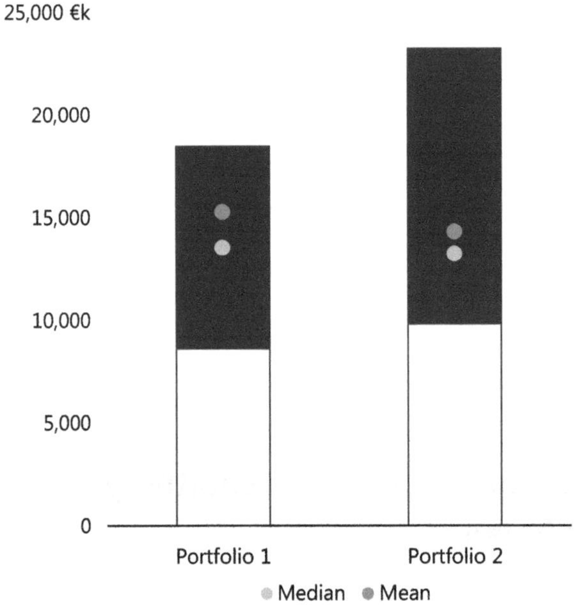

Figure 6: Market risk capital requirements estimated by banks for hypothetical portfolios[(a)]
Source: BCBS (2013a) and BCBS Secretariat calculations.
(a) Range of capital requirements estimated by 17 internationally active banks spanning nine jurisdictions, for two hypothetical diversified portfolios.

can be clearly understood by supervisors, banks and market participants. The consequences of undue complexity can directly affect banks' own internal risk management:

- A bank's board and senior management may find it challenging to fully understand the bank's underlying risk profile and, as a result, the key drivers of the capital framework, even though the public has a legitimate expectation that they have that ability, and they are under a legal obligation to do so. Undue regulatory complexity can therefore impair the ability of the board and senior management of a bank to ensure that the bank has adequate capital to support its risks.
- The use of highly complex approaches can jeopardise sound internal risk management to the extent that bank management places undue reliance on them. Risk management decisions based entirely on the output of complex quantitative analysis may not result in effective and prudent decision-making. More complex frameworks increase "quant risk," whereby risk managers and supervisors effectively delegate key aspects of risk management and supervisory oversight to a limited number of quantitative analysts.

- Compliance with an unduly complex capital framework absorbs a large amount of banks' resources. While this may be manageable for larger institutions, it places a greater burden on other banks.

In short, we know that the pre-crisis framework resulted in imprudently low capital requirements for market risk. We know that market risk represents a very small share of total capital requirements for most banks. We know that the estimated impact of the revised framework appears to be relatively manageable for most banks. So have we placed too much emphasis on attaining "perfect" risk sensitivity, at the expense of simplicity and comparability (not to mention the significant costs associated with development and implementation)?

This brings me to my third point, which is the importance of having a framework that can be realistically implemented by banks and jurisdictions. In postponing its implementation date, GHOS members reaffirmed that they expect the framework's full, timely and consistent implementation. To meet this expectation, the framework needs to be designed in a way that can be implemented by internationally active banks and adequately overseen by supervisors. So while there may be sound conceptual reasons for pursuing a specific approach or making a particular revision to the market risk framework, it is in no one's interest to end up with a framework that cannot be adequately implemented.

The Committee's experience with its market risk QIS is telling. The Committee has conducted many quantitative exercises on market risk, both before and after the publication of the market risk framework, with a QIS exercise currently under way.[4] While the quality of data submitted by banks has improved over time, concerns about data quality remain. Thus, a significant proportion of banks' data has been excluded from the Committee's analysis. These deficiencies may simply reflect the gradual adjustment of banks' systems to the revised framework. But as a result, the Committee has in some areas been left with only a small sample of banks to finalise certain outstanding revisions. This points to the importance of banks providing complete and robust trading book data submissions for the current QIS exercise as well as providing concrete evidence to the questions posed in the consultation to facilitate the standard's finalisation.[5]

So where does this leave us? I'll make three concluding remarks:

- The revised market risk framework will represent a major improvement to the pre-crisis regulatory framework. The framework will address many of the

4 This includes two risk-weighted asset variability studies and twice-yearly capital monitoring data collections.

5 These relate to the treatment of FX risk; trading seasonality as part of the non-modellable risk factor framework; and idiosyncratic equity risk.

fault lines exposed by the global financial crisis. The main elements of the revised framework completed in 2016 are in a stable shape, and the Committee is focused on finalising the few remaining outstanding issues in a timely manner this year.
- In doing so, an important consideration for the Committee is whether the framework adequately balances simplicity, comparability and risk sensitivity. Will the Committee need to consider whether simpler and more robust approaches should be included in the revised market risk framework? This is an open question at this stage, but it's the one which I encourage all stakeholders to take into account.
- There is a clear expectation for full, timely and consistent implementation of the Basel III standards. This includes the January 1, 2022 implementation date of the market risk framework, as reaffirmed in March 2018 by the G20 Finance Ministers and Central Bank Governors (G20 [2018]). So the Committee will increasingly be focused on meeting this expectation.

References

Basel Committee on Banking Supervision (2010): *Basel III: A global regulatory framework for more resilient banks and banking systems*, December.
— (2012): *Fundamental review of the trading book – consultative document*, May
— (2013a): "Analysis of risk-weighted assets for market risk", *Regulatory Consistency Assessment Programme (RCAP)*, January and December.
— (2013b): *The regulatory framework: balancing risk sensitivity, simplicity and comparability*, July 2013.
— (2015): *Fundamental review of the trading book – interim impact analysis*, November
— (2016): *Minimum capital requirements for market risk*, January.
— (2017): *Basel III: finalising post-crisis reforms*, December.
— (2018a): *Basel III monitoring report*, March.
— (2018b): *Revisions to the minimum capital requirements for market risk*, March.
Group of 20 (2018): "Communiqué of Finance Ministers and Central Bank Governors", Buenos Aires, 20 March.
Ingves, S (2015): "From the Vasa to the Basel framework: The dangers of instability", November.

Andreas Dombret, Member, Executive Board, Deutsche Bundesbank (May 2010-May 2018), Member, Board of Directors, Bank for International Settlements, Basel

Basel III: A strong foundation for a thriving economy

Introduction

Haste makes waste. If that is true, Basel III must be one of the most efficient frameworks in the history of global governance. After roughly a decade of analysis, design, debate and revision, on December 7, 2017, the finalisation of the Basel III framework was conclusively agreed.

It is one of the crucial instruments to make the global financial system more resilient following the worst financial crisis since the 1930s.

This chapter will begin with an evaluation of these reforms from a European perspective. It will also highlight that, while the finalisation of Basel III might be the last milestone of the post-crisis reform agenda, nevertheless, one final step remains to get to the goal: implementation of the standard. This will be crucial in deciding whether the agreement will be a lasting success. The chapter will also discuss the challenges of implementing Basel III around the globe; however, focus will be on implementation in the European Union.

A balanced milestone achievement

The Basel III finalisation package is a highly important and, in this day and age, rare global policy cooperation achievement – in light of current political tensions, a global minimum standard is a crucial (and noteworthy) success. Basel III will contribute to stabilising the global financial system and prevent regulatory arbitrage.

Basel III finalisation in a nutshell[1]

Basel III was a mammoth project, lasting from 2009 to 2017. Each of its numerous pieces was necessary to close gaps revealed by the financial crisis.

1 For a detailed description, see Deutsche Bundesbank (2018), Finalising Basel III, Monthly Report, January, 73–89.

https://doi.org/10.1515/9783110621495-003

The process can be split into two phases. During the first phase of Basel III, the focus was largely on the capital side of the capital ratio, that is, the numerator; in contrast, during the second phase – the Basel III finalisation package, which was agreed on December 7, 2017 – regulators concentrated on the calculation of risk-weighted assets (RWAs), that is, the denominator. This was necessary in order to restore the credibility of the calculation of RWAs and improve the comparability of banks' capital ratios. The financial crisis, and analyses performed by the Basel Committee on Banking Supervision (BCBS), had revealed that banks' internal risk calculations and the subsequent regulatory minimum capital requirements were prone to several shortcomings: calculations for similar portfolios could lead to quite different capital requirements, models could be gamed by banks, and some of the inputs prescribed by supervisors also turned out to be less than optimal.

That's why the Basel Committee both enhanced the risk sensitivity of the standardised approaches and constrained internal models, not only through the output floor but also through several input floors and methodological requirements – and this was done across the most important risk categories: these being credit risk, market risk and operational risk.[2] Most prominent among the changes is the output floor of 72.5%, which means that the capital benefit that a bank can gain from using an internal risk measurement model cannot exceed 27.5% of the capital requirement computed solely using the standardised approaches.

However, the Basel III finalisation package also included further the following important addenda:

- The additional leverage ratio requirement for global systemically important banks (G-SIBs)
- Renewal of International Financial Reporting Standard (IFRS) 9 (not part of the Basel III finalisation package, but discussed simultaneously in the Basel Committee)
- The securitisation framework (likewise not part of the Basel III finalisation package, but discussed simultaneously in the Basel Committee)
- Interest rate risk in the banking book (likewise not part of the Basel III finalisation package, but discussed simultaneously in the Basel Committee)

Unfortunately, however, no consensus could be found on ending the privileged treatment of sovereign exposures. I will discuss this in the next section.

In sum, the entire Basel III process has been quite protracted, but its outcome has been a success story. The final version of Basel III restricts or abolishes the

2 Ibid.

use of internal models where reasonable and reduces the unwarranted RWA variability; however, Basel III remains in essence a risk-sensitive approach.

The effects of Basel III

The Basel Committee did find a healthy compromise that will benefit global financial stability and the global economy more generally. For this purpose, the objective of not significantly increasing the minimum capital requirements – a G20-approved guidance – was reached at a global level, but not for Europe (see Table 1).

With an output floor set at 72.5%, especially global systemically important institutions (G-SIIs) will be asked to back their risks with more capital. And, while I understand the challenges facing bigger banks, the increase is manageable and justifiable as it reflects risks in banks' books that should be covered. Moreover, requirements will remain largely unchanged for small- and medium-sized banks, and many small institutions will even see capital savings.

Furthermore, due to the long phase-in period and thanks to the institutions' solid capital base, the expected increases in minimum capital requirements will be manageable for them.

In sum, European banks can cope with the effects and have sufficient room for manoeuvre to undertake the necessary strategic adjustments in light of the structural adjustment process taking place in the banking sector.

One particular point to be stressed is that fears of a possible collateral damage to the economy are, by and large, unsubstantiated.

The first Basel III package was panned by the financial sector as being detrimental to the global economy, as it would undermine lending by banks and thereby lead to deeper recession. These concerns have proven to be demonstrably false. Independent research has clearly shown that increased capital requirements do not lead to less credit supply. Rather, it tends to lead to safer banks, a more stable financial system and can even lead to higher credit provisioning, because banks engage in less risky business activities – such as trading.[3]

3 Admati, A & Hellwig, M (2013), The bankers' new clothes: What's wrong with banking and what to do about it, Princeton University Press, Princeton; Admati, A R; DeMarzo, P M; Hellwig, M & Pfleiderer, P (2010), 'Fallacies, irrelevant facts, and myths in the discussion of capital regulation: Why bank equity is not expensive', Preprints of the Max Planck Institute for Research on Collective Goods, No. 2010, 42; Buch, C M & Prieto, E (2014), 'Do better capitalized banks lend less? Long-run panel evidence from Germany', International Finance 17(1), 1–23; Abbassi, P, Iyer, R, Peydró, J-L and Tous, F R (2016), Banks that trade securities grant fewer loans. Research Brief | 3rd edition – April 2016.

Table 1: Regulatory capital ratios, leverage ratios and capital shortfalls.

	Risk-weighted CET1 capital ratio (%)				Tier 1 leverage ratio (%)			Capital shortfalls (EUR, billions)		
Bank category	No. of banks	Current (Dec 2015)	Revised	Difference	Current (Dec 2015)	Revised	Tier 1 surplus (EUR billions)	CET1	Tier 1 combined[a]	Total capital
All banks	88	12.3	11.6	−0.6	4.8	4.8	1.3	17.5	34.4	39.7
Group 1	36	12.2	11.5	−0.7	4.7	4.8	1.2	16.4	32.0	36.7
G-SIIs	12	11.7	10.9	−0.8	4.5	4.5	0.7	16.4	30.0	36.7
Group 2	52	12.5	12.6	0.2	5.3	5.3	2.3	1.1	2.4	3.0

Source: European Banking Authority, Ad hoc cumulative impact assessment of the Basel reform package.
Note: The column "Tier 1 surplus" shows the Tier 1 capital, as of December 2015, which banks hold above the revised required leverage ratio standard stand-alone (i.e., in isolation from the risk-based requirements), including the G-SIB surcharge, where applicable, as a percentage or leverage ratio exposure. The "Capital shortfalls" column shows the overall capital shortfalls resulting from the combined impact of the requirements.
[a] "Tier 1 combined" shows the overall capital shortfall in Common Equity Tier 1 Capital and T 1 capital instruments.

Moreover, an extensive impact assessment has demonstrated that the Basel III reform package of 2010 had negligible effects on growth, but tremendous positive effects on stability.[4]

Higher requirements thus did indeed reduce the threat of another very costly financial crisis, yet at the same time without affecting the financing of the real economy negatively – the doomsday scenarios painted during the finalisation of Basel III in 2016 and 2017 are thus most likely to be just as false as those in 2010.

The low likelihood of negative repercussions becomes even clearer if we take a look at the expected capital shortfall (see Table 1). Even though concerns about a credit crunch were voiced back when the initial phase of the Basel III reforms was wrapped up in 2010, they never materialised. And that phase revolved around raising a colossal €277 billion of additional capital for Europe's then-undercapitalised banks, compared with a figure of €17.5 billion today.

And the already mentioned 10-year phase-in period will give credit institutions sufficient time to build up capital. Supervisors now have the task of arranging the transition in a way that enables credit institutions to calmly adjust to the new regime.

In sum, then, Basel III is a well-balanced regulatory reform that will improve banks' risk measurement, and thereby help enhance financial stability. Rather than undermining growth, it will prove to be a strong foundation for the global and EU economies, as stable banks will lend more, rather than less, and as banking crises will become less likely.

Full implementation is key

When talking about Basel III, many banks or lobbyists may be hoping for of a less strict implementation of the Basel standards. But a less-than full implementation would be problematic. Instead, all Basel Committee member jurisdictions must do everything in their power to ensure full implementation.

The value of the Basel standards would be much diminished if states were to cherry-pick what parts to implement or if they were to implement a diluted version of the standards. That was ultimately what happened with Basel II, which was fully implemented in neither the United States nor the EU. The United States only implemented those sections that suited it. Because the EU implemented a

4 Macroeconomic Assessment Group (2010), Assessing the macroeconomic impact of the transition to stronger capital and liquidity requirements. Report, Bank for International Settlements.

toothless form of the Basel I floor, the precursor to the output floor, European credit institutions have been disproportionately hard hit now that Basel III has been finalised, accounting for almost two-thirds of the global capital shortfall of just under €28 billion.

What's even more problematic is that a systematic cause lies at the root of the incomplete and at times lax implementation – one that could become virulent again. Banks could be too influential in affecting the implementation, by lobbying politicians. If legislators have learned from the financial crisis, this state of affairs will hopefully not recur.

All 28 jurisdictions involved should therefore transpose Basel III into national or European law in full and as quickly as possible, as this will give credit to institution's certainty.

Basel standards are minimum standards for internationally active banks

But as important as Basel III is, we should not forget what it was made for – and what not. The Basel III standards are, first, *minimum standards* for, second, *internationally active banks*.

Since Basel standards are minimum standards, a country may decide to set stricter requirements. For example, Switzerland has a higher leverage ratio. Another example is the United Kingdom, which has ring-fencing rules in place that separate vital basic functions of a bank from the riskier ones. This policy is not of the Basel Committee's making, and the United Kingdom is free to apply it in its jurisdiction.

The second qualification of the Basel III standard is that it is for internationally active banks. As such, jurisdictions are free to apply a different set of rules to smaller, only nationally active banks that pose no threat to international financial stability.

Many nations already have less restrictive rules on smaller banks in order to reduce the operational burden for them.[5] I am a strong proponent of extending this proportionality further, because the highly complex regulatory reforms after the financial crisis were sought for global banks, and they risk overburdening smaller, regional banks.

---

5 A P C Carvalho, S Hohl, R Raskopf and S Ruhnau (2017) Proportionality in banking regulation: a cross-country comparison. FSI Insights on Policy Implementation No 1.

In sum, then, we should focus on regulating globally active banks, while leaving it up to each individual jurisdiction to regulate locally active banks.

Implementation in the EU

The EU should be pioneering the implementation of the Basel III finalisation package and should be a role model for other jurisdictions. This will not be easy, however, as elections to the European Parliament will take place in mid-2019 and a new College of Commissioners will be appointed after that. We must nonetheless start the process in 2018, so that we do not have to start from scratch at the end of 2019.

The two qualifications of Basel standards, mentioned above, should guide the following implementation efforts:

- The Basel III finalisation package should be fully implemented for internationally active banks
- For smaller, only regionally active institutions, with low-risk profiles, the EU should enhance proportionality in banking regulation, exempting them from certain regulatory requirements in order to reduce operational burdens is one way to achieve this goal

For internationally active banks, implementation must take place with no watering-down of the rules. These banks' assets make up the overwhelming majority of European assets, which is why not softening the Basel III standards for these institutions is of crucial importance for the stability of the European economy.

The EU should see the introduction of Basel III as a catalyst for completing the banking union. A stable euro area needs a strong banking union, and the banking union requires high EU-wide regulatory and supervisory standards. That naturally includes eliminating any legacy problems such as non-performing loans as well as abolishing the preferential treatment of sovereign bonds, which is extremely important for the European monetary union.[6]

In light of Europe's high dependence on the banking sector and the sovereign-bank nexus, the adequate regulatory treatment of sovereign exposures is of particular importance – which means that they cannot continue to have a simple zero-risk weight in future. Unfortunately, the Basel Committee did not find a consensus to initiate a new framework for sovereign exposures. Given that the

6 A Dombret (2018) Now or later? Completing the European banking union. Lecture given at the Graduate Institute Geneva, 20 February 2018.

eurozone crisis was exacerbated by massive sovereign exposures in banks' books, the European Commission's recently communicated plan not to touch preferential treatment means that we have probably missed an opportunity to improve financial stability.

A future euro area crisis would become less likely if ending the privileged treatment of sovereign exposures were one of the first steps in the process of reforming the EU banking union.[7]

The second principle that should guide implementation in the EU is enhancing proportionality. The reasons for the high importance of this issue in the EU are grounded in history: in the EU, international standards since Basel I have been applied to all banks. In this sense, we have a single rulebook for the EU that is designed to guarantee a level playing field. That's one side – the polished side – of the coin. On the flip side – the tarnished side, so to speak – this unity has come at much too high a cost to smaller- and medium-sized institutions ever since Basel II.

The Basel III reforms have made it even harder for these banks, as the rules are getting more and more complicated and explicit, and the list just keeps getting longer. This is increasing the compliance workload – that is, the effort associated with meeting the requirements as well as demonstrating that they have been met. In fact, these rules are well suited to the lion's share of increasingly complicated banking business – but the reality is that not all banks and savings banks have as complex a setup as is assumed under the new framework.

There are two approaches via which this could be achieved in the EU. First, we could take a small-scale approach and introduce simplifications and exceptions to individual rules. Second, we could create a whole new framework – a small banking box – that is specifically tailored to small banks and low-risk institutions. The second solution would be further-reaching and clear-cut. It promises a better cost-benefit ratio in terms of increased efficiency and higher stability.

However, at present – that is, in the context of reviewing the Capital Requirements Regulation (CRR II) and Directive (CRD V) – both of which include some of the outstanding elements of the earlier Basel III package – majority opinion in Europe appears to lean towards the small-scale solution. But, given that we have a long-term time horizon to implement the finalisation package, it would be advisable to revisit the systematic approach of a small banking box. Our concern, however, is not about a specific name or a specific form – the goal is a significant lowering of operational burdens through a systematic, rather than a patchy approach.

7 Ibid.

Conclusion

Basel III has all the potential to be a strong foundation for a thriving economy. The long process in the Basel Committee to finalise the Basel III package has led to a balanced framework that increases stability in the banking sector without significantly increasing capital requirements – from a global perspective – above the levels reached after the 2010 reforms.

But the Basel III framework will be a lasting success only if all BCBS jurisdictions fully transpose the rules into national/jurisdictional law. The EU, but also the United States, should lead this process.

However, after having implemented Basel III, we need a regulatory break – because, yes there is regulatory fatigue. This, though, should not be *carte blanche* for regulatory capture and deregulation. As tired as banks are of new regulation, regulators are just as tired of banks' (often unsolicited) lobbying efforts.

What we need to discuss is how to implement Basel III in a way that is as close to the agreed standards as possible but, at the same time, also reflects national particularities.

Once this has been accomplished, we can take a regulatory break to see how all the reforms interact with each other and whether they are all working as they should.

Michael S. Gibson, Director, Division of Supervision and Regulation, Board of Governors of the Federal Reserve System

An assessment of the Basel III reforms

March 28, 2018

The global financial crisis that began a decade ago caused enormous harm to the well-being of people around the world. In the United States, nearly nine million people lost their jobs in the recession that was triggered by the crisis. It was the most severe economic and financial downturn since the Great Depression.

The crisis revealed serious weaknesses in banks around the world. Many banks failed and others only survived with extraordinary support from governments. Banks had too little capital to support the risks they were taking, too little liquidity to survive a stress scenario and inadequate risk management systems to control their risks. The standards of bank regulation and supervision in effect before the crisis were clearly not sufficient to address these weaknesses.

In response to the crisis, regulators around the world took steps to strengthen bank capital standards. The initial set of reforms, introduced in 2010 and known as "Basel III," increased both the quantity and quality of regulatory capital. In 2013, the United States federal banking agencies finalised a capital rule that, for internationally active banks, aligned with the Basel III standards.[1]

These and other reforms have greatly strengthened the banking system and made the economy more resilient. Notably, large banking firms in the United States have more than doubled their capital positions from where they stood before the crisis.[2]

In December 2017, additional measures were added to the Basel III reforms to improve the risk sensitivity of the capital requirements, reduce the variability in regulatory capital across banks and promote a level playing field among internationally

1 "Federal Reserve Board approves final rule to help ensure banks maintain strong capital positions," 2 July 2013, https://www.federalreserve.gov/newsevents/pressreleases/bcreg20130702a.htm.

2 "Federal Reserve releases results of Comprehensive Capital Analysis and Review (CCAR)," 28 June 2017. https://www.federalreserve.gov/newsevents/pressreleases/bcreg20170628a.htm

Notes: Director, Division of Supervision and Regulation, Federal Reserve Board. These remarks were presented at the conference "Basel III: Are We Done Now?" organised by the Institute for Law and Finance, Goethe University, Frankfurt am Main, January 29, 2018. These remarks reflect my own views and do not necessarily represent the views of other members of the staff or the Board of Governors.

https://doi.org/10.1515/9783110621495-004

active banks. The United States federal banking agencies have publicly announced their support for the agreement to finalise the additional Basel III reforms.[3]

The December 2017 reforms include important measures to constrain the use of bank internal models in setting capital requirements. In particular, the package contains an output floor based on standardised capital requirements to reduce risk-weighted asset variability across banks and to guard against excessively low risk-based capital requirements. The standardised floor will be an important prudential measure that will protect global financial stability and bolster the market's confidence in the banking industry. The package also includes disclosure of standardised risk-weighted assets to enhance market discipline.

Assessment

The topic of today's panel discussion is an assessment of the Basel III reforms. These reforms are multi-faceted and an assessment can have many dimensions. The most important dimension, where I will focus my remarks, is the ability of the reforms to limit the undesirable variation in risk-weighted assets when the risk weights are based on bank internal models. Another important dimension that I will comment on is the complexity of the reforms. Of course, at this early stage, any assessment must necessarily be preliminary until the reforms have been implemented and enough time has elapsed to observe their effects.

A key objective of the December 2017 reforms is to limit the undesirable variation in risk-weighted assets caused by bank internal models. The capital requirements that were developed in the decade before the financial crisis, known as Basel II, had an admirable goal: to make regulatory capital requirements more risk sensitive. However, once the Basel II requirements began to be implemented, it became clear that Basel II gave banks too much freedom to set capital requirements with their own models. Banks used this freedom to game the system by changing their models with the express purpose of reducing their capital requirements, rather than measuring their risks better.[4]

Even when banks may not have been consciously gaming the system, the freedom to use their own models allows banks to assign different risk weights,

---

3 "U.S. banking agencies support conclusion of reforms to international capital standards," 7 December 2017. https://www.federalreserve.gov/newsevents/pressreleases/bcreg20171207

4 For one example in the public domain, see Senate Permanent Subcommittee on Investigations, 2013, JPMorgan Chase whale trades: A case history of derivatives risks and abuses, http://www.hsgac.senate.gov/download/?id=F2B1E62B-0B68-4977-BF6A-025695C60897.

and thus hold different capital, for the same exposures. If these differences were small and distributed evenly across banks, they might be acceptable, but evidence shows that they are neither.

The Basel Committee studied one aspect of the variability in risk-weighted assets across banks in a 2013 paper.[5] The paper compared risk weights from bank internal models for wholesale credit exposures to sovereigns, banks and corporates across 32 large, internationally active banks. The comparison was made across identical exposures – that is, risk weights were compared where more than one bank had lent money to the same borrower.

Differences in risk-weighted assets across banks can be desirable, if they reflect true underlying differences in the risk across banks' portfolios. For example, a bank that lends to high-risk borrowers should have higher risk-weighted assets than a bank that lends to low-risk borrowers, holding other things constant. However, the Basel Committee's study controlled for differences in portfolio risk by measuring differences in risk weights for *exposures to the same borrowers*. All of this latter variability is by definition undesirable and makes it difficult or impossible to compare the adequacy of capital levels across banks.

The Basel Committee's study found that banks were choosing remarkably different risk weights for exposures to identical borrowers. The variation in internally modelled risk weights was so great that the reported capital ratio for a bank with a benchmark risk-based capital ratio of 10% holding these types of wholesale exposures could vary by as much as 2 percentage points in either direction, a 20% difference in relative terms. In other words, a bank whose true risk-based capital ratio was 10% could report a capital ratio between 8% and 12%. The excessive variation in internally modelled risk weights, as documented by the Basel Committee's study, and many other studies, was a key motivation for the December 2017 Basel III reforms.[6]

Several elements of the Basel III reforms will address the excessive variability in risk-weighted assets derived from bank internal models. For some exposures, it will no longer be permitted to use bank internal models to set risk weights. For other exposures, a bank's flexibility to choose the parameters of internal models will be constrained. And, an output floor based on standardised capital requirements will be introduced. This floor, set at 72.5% of the standardised capital

5 Basel Committee on Banking Supervision, 2013, Regulatory consistency assessment programme (RCAP) – Analysis of risk-weighted assets for credit risk in the banking book, http://www.bis.org/publ/bcbs256.pdf.

6 For an additional study of variability in risk-weighted assets, see Simon Samuels, 2012, Why markets do not trust Basel II Internal Ratings-Based Approach: What can be done about it?, Journal of Risk Management in Financial Institutions 6:1, 10–22.

requirement, will limit the reduction in capital requirements that outlier banks can achieve with internally modelled risk weights. Together, these measures should reduce the undesirable excessive variability in risk-weighted assets based on bank internal models.

These measures are certainly a step in the right direction to reduce excessive variability in risk-weighted assets caused by bank internal models. Whether these measures are enough to restore the market's confidence in banks' reported risk-weighted assets is uncertain and still to be determined. These reforms must be implemented over the coming years and take effect before a full evaluation can be made.

Supervisory stress testing is another post-crisis addition to bank supervision and regulation that helps to limit the problems caused by using bank internal models to set risk-weighted assets. In the United States, and several other jurisdictions, supervisors regularly conduct a stress test of large banking firms to assess whether these firms have enough capital to weather a severe recession and continue to be able to lend to households and businesses. The Federal Reserve's stress test relies on detailed data that large banks submit on their exposures, including loan-level data for selected wholesale and retail exposures. Importantly, the Federal Reserve uses its own independent models to estimate stressed losses, revenues and capital ratios under a severely adverse macroeconomic scenario, which helps to ensure the capital adequacy of the largest banking firms in a risk-sensitive way that is largely independent of bank internal models (and regulatory risk weights).[7]

Another concern that has been raised regarding bank capital standards – secondary to risk-weighted asset variability but still important – is their complexity. As Haldane and Madouros (2012) have argued persuasively, one reason why capital regulation failed to prevent the financial crisis was its growing complexity.[8] The growing complexity of the financial system had prompted regulators to adopt ever more complex rules, such as Basel II. But a growing amount of theory and empirical evidence suggests that complex rules may not be as robust as simple rules when facing complex banks and financial instruments.

One particularly harmful consequence of the complex rules, and how the rules interacted with the growing complexity of large banks, was that capital calculations became more opaque. As a result, before the crisis, it became harder to audit or check a bank's regulatory capital calculations; it also became harder for

7 Public disclosure of the stress test scenarios and results also contributes to market discipline on bank risk-taking.

8 See Haldane, Andrew and Vasileios Madouros, 2012, The dog and the frisbee, Bank of England working paper, https://www.bis.org/review/r120905a.pdf.

a bank to explain how changes in its balance sheet or business activities affected its capital position.

The Basel Committee itself has recognised the downside of complex rules.[9] In a recent paper, the Basel Committee described the evolution of the regulatory capital framework and the ways in which complexity has increased over time while comparability across firms and over time has declined. The paper questions whether the balance of simplicity, comparability and risk sensitivity in bank capital requirements should be reconsidered.

My preliminary assessment, which will of course have to be updated as the Basel III reforms are implemented, is that the reforms have not done much to reduce complexity. The Basel III reforms do contain an improved standardised approach to operational risk, which will be simpler than the previous internal model-based approach. The new standardised approach to credit risk has added more buckets and risk drivers, making it more complex than the previous standardised approach. The new constraints on bank internal models will make the internal rating-based approaches to credit risk more complex, not less. An output floor based on the new standardised risk weights will be an easily understood way to build confidence in banks' capital calculations but will not simplify those calculations.

Overall, the Basel III rules still seem quite complex. In my view, further limits on the role of bank internal models offer the best prospect for reducing the complexity of capital requirements, with risk sensitivity maintained through supervisory stress testing.

Conclusion

The Basel III reforms and a robust supervisory stress test, working together, represent a significant and valuable regulatory realignment and response to the financial crisis. These measures have addressed some of the shortcomings of the pre-crisis regulatory capital regime, in particular the excessive variability in risk-weighted assets based on bank internal models. Strong regulatory capital standards that help to maintain the safety and soundness of the largest banks are fundamental to maintaining the stability of the financial system and the broader economy.

9 Basel Committee on Banking Supervision, 2013, The regulatory framework: balancing risk sensitivity, simplicity and comparability – discussion paper, http://www.bis.org/publ/bcbs258.pdf.

III: Basel III: sense and sensitivity, a thematic overview

Sabine Lautenschläger, Member of the Executive Board & Vice-Chair of the Supervisory Board of the European Central Bank

It is done: Basel III has been finalised

I admit that it was a long journey, but in my view, it was worth the wait: Basel III will help to make banking safer. It is now crucial, though, that Basel III is properly implemented – in Europe and around the world. It must not be watered down.

Basel III marks the end of the post-crisis reforms; regulatory certainty has been restored. The banks know what awaits them; they can be confident about the regulatory framework, and can plan ahead and support the real economy.

But does Basel III deliver what was promised? Does it, on the one hand, create rules which are sufficiently risk sensitive to set the right incentives for banks? And does it, on the other hand, create rules which are simple enough to decrease model risk?

Banks are not enchanted by Basel III. Many of them claim that it throws risk sensitivity overboard and penalises low-risk exposures. Are these claims justified?

Well, we have not thrown risk sensitivity overboard. And why would we? Risk sensitivity helps align capital requirements with actual levels of risk and supports an efficient capital allocation. It inhibits arbitrage and risk shifting. And risk-sensitive rules promote sound risk management.

But we all know how challenging it is to measure and model risks. Much depends on the quality of the models; much depends on the data and the assumptions that feed into those models; and much depends on supervisors' capacity to act. If there are errors along the way, banks might end up undercapitalised and vulnerable. This, in turn, might lead markets to question the reliability of risk-based capital requirements in general, which would undermine trust in banks more generally.

Therefore we need to balance risk sensitivity with some safeguards. And this is exactly what we aim to do with Basel III. It preserves risk sensitivity. It retains internal models for most asset classes. And it enhances the risk sensitivity of the standardised approaches. But at the same time, Basel III adds a few safeguards.

First, I think we can all agree that it makes no sense to allow for more complex risk-sensitive capital requirements if risks cannot be measured and modelled. Basel III therefore aligns the degree of risk sensitivity with the extent to which it is possible to measure and model risks.[1]

---

1 For example, modelling will no longer be permitted for operational risk. And under the internal ratings-based approach for credit risk, it will not be possible to model "loss given default" for certain low-default portfolios.

https://doi.org/10.1515/9783110621495-005

Second, there are some more conservative haircuts on collateral and some input floors. These input floors lie beneath the parameters for "probability of default" and "loss given default." And there will be floors beneath the "exposure at default" calculation as well. These floors work bottom-up; they will keep banks from feeding their internal models with excessively low inputs. This serves as a safeguard as it prevents capital requirements from being set too low.

And, yes, these input floors make the rules a bit less risk sensitive. But we need to look at this in absolute terms – for residential mortgages, the input floor increases from three basis points to five basis points. Five basis points correspond to a once-in-2,000 years default rate! Is such a floor really too conservative? At global level, the bottom-up reforms see small increases in capital for exposures to other banks, large corporates and equity investments. This is somewhat offset by a reduction in risk weights for loans to small- and medium-sized enterprises.

Third, there is the hotly debated output floor. It ensures that risk-weighted assets calculated with internal models do not fall too far below those calculated with standardised approaches. "Too far below" means they must reach at least 72.5%. Does that kill risk sensitivity? No, it does not. Obviously, there is still room for banks to apply individual risk weights and to benefit from lower capital requirements for classic, low-risk banking business.

And more than that: the effective floor might even be lower than 72.5%. This is due to the fact that many banks apply the standardised approaches to at least some exposures. This implies that, depending on the share of assets still under the standardised approach, the effective floor for them could be lower than 72.5%.

At the same time, Basel III makes the standardised approaches themselves more risk sensitive. One example is residential mortgages. Under Basel II, the standardised approach assigned the same risk weight to almost all such mortgages. But in Basel III, the risk weights of residential mortgages depend on the loan-to-value ratios. The output floor is thus set in relation to a benchmark, which itself has become more risk sensitive. And it should not be forgotten that, in some cases, the standardised approaches have become less costly in terms of capital. At global level, the capital requirements from standardised approaches have been reduced by about 2% on average. Mortgages and corporate lending make up the majority of these reductions.

So, Basel III does keep risk sensitivity on board. It acknowledges, though, that there are limits to internal models. It provides safeguards to restore trust in risk-based capital requirements.

Does this mean that Basel III is the perfect standard – the philosopher's stone of banking regulation?

Well, Basel III is a global standard, and across the world, financial sectors differ greatly. Just think of real-estate financing and how differently it is treated in Europe compared with the United States. Thus, a global standard cannot suit everyone perfectly. The key is to find an acceptable compromise; the alternative would be to have no global standard, and that would definitely be worse. The output floor in particular is one such compromise.

What impact will the final Basel III package have on banks – and on their business models and their capital?

The rules are not neutral. The bottom-up safeguards in Basel III, including the input floors, will have more impact on risk weights in some business areas. Certain retail credit card exposures are one example. On the other hand, the top–down output floor affects overall capital requirements, depending on the overall portfolio composition of a bank. For example, our analysis suggests that the difference between internal ratings-based and standardised risk weights tend to be relatively large in certain segments of real-estate markets where historical loss rates are exceptionally low. The output floor tends to be more binding for banks that are heavily engaged in these markets.

Overall, it is hard to predict how business models will evolve. This depends not only on regulation, but also on many other factors, including the future path of profitability in different business areas, the pricing power banks have, and, eventually, how banks will adapt their business models.

Now what about additional capital requirements? What about the banks' claim that the burden might be too heavy for them? There are two things to bear in mind.

First, there will be a long transition period. This is at the heart of the overall compromise that paved the way for finalising Basel III. This transition period runs right through to 2027. It gives banks and legislators time to implement all the changes introduced by Basel III.

Second, the European Banking Authority estimates that, for EU banks, the final Basel III package will lead to an aggregate Tier 1 capital shortfall of €34.4 billion. Is that a lot? In 2016, the largest banks in the euro area earned €50 billion – net, after taxes, and in a difficult environment. Also, the capital shortfall refers to the end of the transition period, which is 9 years away. Most banks should be able to earn their way out of potential shortfalls.

To sum up, Basel III preserves risk sensitivity in a sensible way. At the same time, banks will be able to handle its impact and, in the long run, they too will benefit from a more stable banking system.

Paul Hilbers, Director Financial Stability at the Netherlands Bank and Professor at Nyenrode Business University

Basel III: We are almost there; the key challenge now is implementation

Introduction

Let me start by saying that the Basel Committee has done a tremendous job over the past decade in drawing lessons from the crisis and, more importantly, developing a new post-crisis international standard for banking regulation and supervision, named Basel III. (BCBS, 2017a). This process took a while. In the summer of 2009 new trading book and securitisation rules came about. This was sometimes referred to as Basel 2.5 and was really the first reaction to the crisis. The major piece then came in December 2010 with the Basel III Accord, which was subsequently endorsed by the Governors and Heads of Supervision (GHOS) in early 2011. Important new elements were the rules regarding the quality of capital, the ratios for CET1, T1 and total capital, and of course the various buffers: the capital conservation buffer, the countercyclical buffer and the buffer for global systemically important banks (G-SIBs). Plus, new standards for liquidity: the LCR and the NSFR. The Accord also included a leverage ratio that would migrate later to pillar 1.

In my contribution, I will focus on three elements of the Basel III package: its completeness (are we done yet?), its direct impact on the banks' capital requirements and the potential longer term effects on the banks' business models. I will end looking ahead, with a focus on sovereign risk and implementation.

1 Completeness of the Basel III package

Are we done?

Already in 2011 we asked ourselves that question: are we done now? So the question asked in this seminar at the Goethe Universität is not a new one. The Basel

Note: The author would like to thank Marco van Hengel and Ron Jongen for their contribution.

https://doi.org/10.1515/9783110621495-006

Accord in 2011 (Basel III) marked the fundamental revision of the framework after the financial crisis to increase the resilience of banks. The follow-up in 2017 (Basel 3.5) further developed and refined this framework with important additional elements.

The 2011 Basel III was all about the quality of capital and the ratio of capital in relation to risk-weighted assets (RWAs). It was concentrated on the numerator, one might say. So what about the denominator, the RWA? Are they determined in the right way? The essence of Basel 3.5 was really focused on that question: could we trust the RWAs, both under the Standardised Approach (SA), but even more so under the Internal Ratings Based (IRB) approach, and what is the room and role for internal models? Clearly, only when these three elements – the quality of capital, the ratio expressed in RWA and the determination of RWA under both SA and IRB – are established correctly, the capital requirement can be adequate. Incidentally, it is interesting to note that the Basel Committee itself refers to the reform process over the period 2009–2017 as Basel III, while the banking industry – given its fundamental nature – often refers to the latest agreement at the end of 2017 as Basel IV. In my country, we refer to the latter as Basel 3.5, seeing it as a finalisation of the Basel III process.

What were the key requirements for determining RWAs?

Basel 3.5 strikes a balance between simplicity, comparability and risk-sensitivity: a more risk-sensitive SA (based on a small set of risk drivers), no more complex modelling of relations that are hard or impossible to model (such as operational risk), input floors and an aggregate output floor and above all less *unwarranted* RWA variation. The latter refers to variations in the RWAs that cannot be attributed to differences in risk (note that *warranted* variation due to differences in risk is fine).

Basel 3.5 also includes another important element, and that is the add-on to the leverage ratio requirement for G-SIBs. This aspect of the package often receives less attention, but is key as well. The leverage ratio is a relatively raw risk-insensitive measure, but is an important backstop. There have been clear links between leverage and banking sector problems in times of crisis. Because of its simplicity, there is less room for window dressing. The leverage ratio is an important backstop for a small country like mine that has a concentrated banking sector, dominated by a few very large banks that dominantly rely on internal models. We would actually have liked a somewhat higher surcharge and also one for domestic systemically important bank (D-SIBs).

Is that all?

Yes and no.

Yes, because the 2017 Accord completes the post-crisis agenda and we can now shift our attention towards implementation.

No, although not part of the Basel 3.5 package, there was also another important paper issued in early December: the discussion paper on sovereign exposures (BCBS, 2017b). Discussions on that issue did not lead to proposals at this stage to make changes, but the discussion paper was put out for comments by March of this year, and in the meantime about 60 reactions have been received by the Committee. I will return to that paper at the end.

2 Impact on the banks of Basel 3.5

As indicated before, the development of the 2017 framework was a follow-up to the fundamental revision in 2011.

At a truly global level – that is to say for all the banking systems of the BCBS membership – and in the aggregate, the impact of the Basel 3.5 package is limited. That is in line with the objective of *no significant overall increase in capital requirements*. The package of Basel 3.5 was meant to make regulations simpler and more comparable, not necessarily higher. However, the impact differs sharply between continents, regions, jurisdictions and certainly between individual banks.

In general one can say that the impact on Europe is generally stronger than that in many other regions. This has in part to do with the characteristics of the EU banking system. Relevant factors why the impact on Europe is stronger are the following. First, EU banks carry more on their books than some banks elsewhere; for example, certain US banks have considerable off-balance-sheet operations and sell off their mortgages to Fannie Mae and Freddie Mac. Second, some EU banks make intensive use of internal models, and are therefore more affected by limitations in the use of models, including input floors and an output floor. Third, Europe has a much more bank-based system of financial intermediation, and furthermore, it rolls out Basel accords over all banks and not just the biggest internationally active ones.

This is certainly not to say that Europe should not implement Basel 3.5 – it should do so fully, timely and consistently – but the impact will be more significant than elsewhere and that is, for example, why the relatively long transition period (until 2027) is essential to avoid disruption.

The impact of Basel 3.5 is also quite strong in my country (DNB, 2017a): a mid-sized, open economy with a relatively large banking system, including one G-SIB. We estimated at the time that the necessary capital increase due to the increase in RWAs is about €14 billion. That is needed to bring the banks to the required capital ratios that make them stable, both within our system and in the international market place. Incidentally, in earlier Basel proposals the impact was more than €50 billion in additional capital, and that would have been clearly disproportional. An important issue concerns our mortgages, which has high loan to value ratios ("LTVs"), but have relatively low default rates, even during the crisis when house prices dropped by 30% in real terms. What you see here is that differences in the structure and functioning of markets between countries can make it difficult to come up with a reasonable global standard and a level playing field.

To put the number of €14 billion in perspective, total CET1 of our major banks currently stands at about €90 billion, so the increase is some 15%. Since annual profits in recent years were about €6 billion, it will take about 2.5 years of retained earnings to reach the required new capital levels, over a period of about a decade. We therefore concluded in a recent DNB press release (DNB, 2017a) that the impact is "significant but manageable." The relatively long transition period is essential to limit disruptions and give banks time to adjust. In the past, the point was made that in practice new Basel capital standards had to be met within a much shorter time frame than prescribed by the Accord. In this case, we believe that this may be much less of an issue, since capital ratios at the outset of Basel 3.5 were much more favourable than those at the outset of, for example, Basel III back in 2010–11.

This brings me to my third point, dealing with the impact on banks' business models.

3 Impact on banks' business models

The analysis above is very much based on a static impact of the Basel accord, that is, the effects refer to the direct impact on banks under unchanged business models. In practice, however, banks will start rethinking their business models in light of Basel 3.5. In fact, most banks have already done so in the years leading up to the Accord based on expectations about the outcome. This was indeed what we have been advising banks to do so in our jurisdiction. For instance, already in 2015 we have pointed out to the banks that they would need to prepare for a different regulatory treatment of (in particular high-LTV) mortgages. This resulted in different pricing and a shift in mortgage loans from the banking sector to insurers and pension funds. Given the long liabilities of the latter, this shift contributed to a better match between assets and liabilities among these institutional investors.

Let me, however, step back a bit and discuss how banks can react in terms of their business models. There are basically two "corner solutions."

The one is that banks can leave their business models unchanged and just "pay the price" of Basel 3.5 in terms of higher capital requirements. That is basically what you see in the results of Quantitative Impact Studies (QISs). This is probably what happens in cases where the impact on banks is relatively limited.

The other extreme is that banks do everything to limit the capital implications of Basel 3.5. That generally means reducing or selling activities that carry an increased RWA and move into areas with lower RWA. But that may have significant implications for their returns as well.

In practice, banks will end up somewhere between these two extremes, adjusting their balance sheet to the changed risk weights (and options to use modelling, which are now limited and – if allowed – subject to input and output floors). However, it is not clear yet where exactly on this line they will end up.

Return on equity (ROE) will probably be lower and that is acceptable

Important, of course, is what Basel 3.5 does to the banks' earnings. Higher capital requirements generally mean lower earnings, since the cost of equity is higher than that of other funding sources (deposits, loans), assuming that Modigliani-Miller does not hold. However, there will also be an impact of the increased resilience and stability of the banks on the cost of equity. So the ROE can be lower in a post Basel 3.5 world, although by how much is not yet easy to establish. Calculations for my country (Daniels et al, 2016) showed that the ROE might end up below 10%, which is clearly lower than in the pre-crisis days, but we have also witnessed what the strong focus on – if not obsession with – a high ROE can bring. The end result of course also depends on market power of banks and the room for cost-cutting measures.

Plus, there are important structural developments in banking that require attention. Fintech is developing rapidly. Banks also need to focus on that. This can actually be a far more significant development for banks' business models and earnings than the increase in capital requirements of Basel 3.5. We are actively engaged in discussions with our banks on these issues.

4 Sovereign risk: an unfinished agenda

Notwithstanding the broad and comprehensive reforms of Basel III, there is a single item where a long-term unfinished agenda remains. This concerns the regulatory treatment of sovereign exposures. Sovereign exposures are an important part of the balance sheet of banks, which have been left untouched since the crisis. It is a complex and delicate discussion that needs to be treated carefully, but we need to keep this on the future agenda and continue to deepen our analysis.

Sovereign debt fulfils an essential role in the financial markets. A well-developed government bond market supports economic development and fiscal policy over the economic cycle. Government bonds are also important in the implementation and transmission of monetary policy. Moreover, government bonds are crucial in the functioning of financial markets in market-making operations, as collateral and as reference rate for pricing other financial assets. Finally, government bonds have a central role in the risk and liquidity management of banks.

At the same time, there are several arguments why the current preferential treatment deserves a revision. Sovereign exposures are not risk free. The current discretion in the standard approach to apply a 0% risk-weighting does not fit well with economic reality that losses on sovereign holdings can and do occur. The underpricing of risk can lead to excessive risk taking. Moreover, it also strengthens the interconnectedness between sovereigns and banks. The "home bias" of banks towards the government debt of their own country can act as a shock absorber during periods of financial stability. However, beyond a certain threshold, the sovereign-bank nexus also creates contagion effects which may undermine financial stability. This diabolic loop was at the core of the European debt crisis.

Further steps in the regulation of sovereign exposures are particularly important within Europe (DNB, 2017b). Countries in a monetary union do not have their own currency and are more vulnerable to confidence crises and solvency problems. Doubts about debt sustainability can lead to capital flight with further increases in yields. During the European debt crisis, the European Central Bank provided ample liquidity and acted as a lender of last resort. However, we should also look to a more structural solution with adequate (non-zero) risk weights and measures to reduce concentration risk. In an integrated European financial market, there is room for reducing concentration by diversifying into different bond markets, without incurring exchange rate risk. Adequate regulation of sovereign exposures would also strengthen the European banking union.

5 Let's now focus on implementation

Basel 3.5 has made an end to a long period of regulatory uncertainty. The banks have been complaining that the ongoing discussions about Basel III made it very difficult for them to develop longer term strategies and make business plans. I think they had a point there. The crisis took place in 2007/2008 and it took the international community about 10 years to finalise its response. At the same time, this was a difficult exercise that had to be accomplished during a period of vast differences between economic circumstances in jurisdictions – compare, for example, the developments in East Asia to those in Europe during this period. All in all, I think the Basel Committee on Banking Supervision can be proud of a comprehensive package. There is now far more stability and regulatory certainty that banks can build upon.

The discussions have been *broad, deep* and *intense*. With the exception of sovereign risk, the reforms have been enough for now and we should move into the phase of implementation and consolidation. Lawmakers need time to introduce new legislation in line with Basel 3.5 and banks need to further adjust their business models. This should be our primary focus. The Basel Committee on Banking Supervision would then – after a decade of almost exclusively focusing on regulation – shift its attention towards the central aspect in its name: banking supervision.

References

BCBS, *Basel III: Finalizing post-crisis reforms*, BIS, December 2017a.

BCBS, *Discussion paper – The regulatory treatment of sovereign exposures*, BIS, December 2017b.

Daniels, Tijmen and Shahin Kamalodin, *The Return on Equity of Large Dutch Banks*, DNB Occasional Study, September 2016.

DNB, DNBulletin: *Basel Committee completes post-crisis bank regulation reforms*, December 2017a.

DNB, DNBulletin: *Call for review of preferential treatment of sovereign exposures in the capital framework*, December 2017b.

Martin Merlin, Director, Regulation and prudential supervision of financial institutions, European Commission

The view from Brussels

The importance of risk sensitivity

Risk sensitivity in the prudential framework for banks is important and needs to be maintained. If well crafted, risk sensitivity helps ensure that credit is allocated efficiently in the economy.

It also encourages good risk management by individual banks and thus can increase financial stability overall. Furthermore, risk sensitivity ensures that certain unique characteristics of specific banks, financial markets and jurisdictions are automatically reflected in banks' prudential requirements.

This last point is of particular importance for Europe, as we – contrary to most other jurisdictions – apply almost the same set of rules to all our banks. In addition, there are certain types of exposure that are prevalent in Europe and that require sufficient risk sensitivity. One example is mortgage loans. European banks tend to hold a large amount of low-risk mortgages on their balance sheets compared to banks in many other jurisdictions. Under the current framework, these loans can and should attract relatively low risk weights in particular if internal models are used – and they often are – to determine these risk weights.

Analyses conducted by the Basel Committee and by the EBA have consistently shown that differences in risk weights between banks are largely justified by differences in underlying risks.

Dealing with unjustified variability in risk weights

That said, the same analyses also showed that some differences in risk weights result from differences in practices between banks and between supervisors, or from situations where a lack of data makes modelling difficult. Much of this variability is probably unjustified and undesirable, as it hinders the comparability of capital ratios and also impacts the level playing field among banks. In some cases, it may even result in insufficient levels of capital held by individual institutions.

There are different ways of tackling this problem of unjustified variability in risk weights. In Europe, we have taken steps to address it within the existing Basel

https://doi.org/10.1515/9783110621495-007

framework: We have created a single rule book with technical standards to harmonise risk measurement, and in the Banking Union, the Single Supervisory Mechanism approves and reviews regulatory capital models in a coherent manner. In addition, the EBA conducts benchmarking exercises every year. We believe that these efforts require strong commitment and significant resources from European regulators, supervisors and banks, but they are effective in addressing unjustified variability in a targeted manner without hampering variability which is justified by the underlying risks.

However, some have argued that the bottom-up approach pursued in Europe was not sufficient and needed to be complemented. Indeed, the Basel Committee took the view that the Basel framework needed revision to somewhat change the balance between risk sensitivity, simplicity and comparability of capital ratios. The Commission has supported this general objective.

However, some initial ideas for reform centred around putting in place very significant constraints on internal modelling, which in many cases would have limited not only unjustified variability, but all variability. Instead of addressing outliers in a targeted manner, as we have been trying to do in Europe, these proposals would have constrained risk sensitivity for large parts of the banking sector and might thus have distorted capital allocation within the European Union (the "EU").

The outcome

Since then, a number of important changes were made to the original plans in order to address the concerns raised by a number of Basel Committee members. These changes included a better treatment of exposures to small and medium-size enterprises as well as a more risk-sensitive treatment of real estate and specialised lending exposures, to name a few of those that were important from the perspective of the EU. The final agreement disallows the use of internal models only in areas where reliable and robust modelling appears difficult to accomplish, which we think is the right outcome. The output floor is now designed and calibrated in a much more sensible way, and therefore we believe that overall the Committee has struck a very good compromise.

In terms of impact, EBA's recent analysis of the final agreement – based on a sample of 88 EU banks – shows that risk sensitivity in the calculation of capital requirements will be maintained for the majority of banks in the EU. The EBA calculated for each bank whether capital requirements were highest if calculated under risk-based capital requirements without the output floor, under the leverage ratio or under the output floor, and the results showed that 58% of banks will be bound by risk-based requirements, 22% by the leverage ratio and 20% by the output floor once the output floor is fully phased-in in 2027. Prior to 2027, more banks will be bound by the leverage ratio but much fewer by the output floor. This leads us to believe that the Committee's work should indeed translate into an appropriate balance between risk sensitivity, simplicity and comparability.

Next steps

What are the next steps at EU level? It is not our intention to merge the EU implementation of the new framework into the currently ongoing EU negotiations on the Commission's "Banking Package," in which we proposed the EU implementation of a number of Basel standards agreed at an earlier stage, but instead we will table a separate proposal.

To this end, we have already launched a public consultation in March, which will soon be followed by a request for advice from the Commission to the EBA. We will use this input to conduct an impact assessment, which will not only look at the impact on banks and their capital requirements, but also at the impact on the wider economy. We expect to be able to table a legislative proposal to implement the new Basel agreement early during the term of the next Commission, probably in early 2020.

The views expressed in the text are the private views of the author and may not, under any circumstances, be interpreted as stating an official position of the European Commission.

Summary

- Risk sensitivity in the prudential framework is important, in particular in Europe.
- In Europe, we have therefore been addressing shortcomings of the current framework in a targeted manner without unduly constraining risk sensitivity.
- In contrast, some of the original reform proposals by the Basel Committee would have constrained risk sensitivity too much, by excessively limiting variability in cases where it is justified by underlying differences in risk.
- The subsequent changes made by the Basel Committee resulted in an agreement which is a good compromise overall, and which should translate into an

appropriate balance between risk sensitivity, simplicity and comparability, as intended.

- The European Banking Authority (the "EBA") estimates that 58% of banks will be bound by risk-based requirements, 22% by the leverage ratio and 20% by the output floor once the output floor is fully phased-in, that is by 2027.
- At EU level, the European Commission (the "Commission") will conduct an impact assessment, with advice from the EBA and responses to our public consultation serving as input. Based on the outcome, the Commission will decide how to implement the agreement.

Patrick Kenadjian, Senior Counsel, Davis Polk & Wardwell LLP

The last round of Basel III and the regulatory trilemma

Why we ended up here

The round of reforms of bank capital adequacy rules known as Basel III commenced in 2009 and for the first part, focusing on the numerator of the capital ratio, was agreed to in principle already in 2011. However, the last round of what regulators continue to call Basel III and many others, including some authors in this volume, have dubbed Basel IV was only concluded in December 2017, a good two years behind the original schedule. This round focused on the denominator of the ratio, the calculation of risk-weighted assets (RWAs). The key point of dispute which led to the delay was the question of how far large banks with sophisticated risk management systems that had obtained the right under Basel II to calculate the risk weights of their own assets based on internal models approved by their supervisors would be allowed to continue to do so in the face of rising doubts as to the comparability of the results obtained by these models.

The notion of internal models had been introduced in Basel II on the theory that these institutions probably knew more about the risks in their portfolios than their supervisors did and that, so long as the models had been vetted by the supervisors, they could be relied upon by the institutions, not only in their internal risk management functions but also in calculating and reporting their RWAs for capital adequacy purposes. This clearly put the supervisors at an informational disadvantage: Once the systems were up and running they took on the character of "black boxes" for outsiders, including the supervisors who had initially approved them, as well as analysts and investors, but it seemed consistent with the idea that greater sensitivity to risk, which was the driving force behind the move to Basel II from Basel I, would provide better calibration of capital to the risks of the business actually being conducted, based on the best available information about those risks that were accumulated by the institutions themselves. Criticism that this constituted an exorbitant privilege, akin to allowing students to grade their own papers, was brushed aside, even though estimates of the savings in RWAs through the use of internal models ran between 5% and 15%.

The banks which had internal models were not required to use them for reporting purposes, they could pick and choose among various asset classes

https://doi.org/10.1515/9783110621495-008

which they would report under their internal model and which they would report under the standardised approach, and it was always assumed that they made their choices based on whichever method gave them a lower risk weight, leading to a certain amount of scepticism about reported numbers. As early as 2012, an IMF Working Paper had documented regional discrepancies in RWA density (i.e., the relationship of RWAs reported by banks to their total balance sheet assets) among North American banks at 57%, Asian banks at 51% and European banks at 35%. (LeLesle, Vanessa and Sofiyya Abramova, Revisiting Risk Weighted Assets, Why do RWAs Differ Across Countries and What Can Be Done About It?, IMF Working Paper, WP12/90, March 2012). But when the Basel Committee started looking into how uniform the results produced by the internal models were in 2013, critics' and sceptics' worst fears appeared to be confirmed. When asked to weight a hypothetical portfolio, the results reported by the banks based on their internal models varied by up to 50%. (Basel Committee on Banking Supervision (BCBS) Analysis of risk-weighted assets for credit risk in the banking book, Regulatory Consistency Assessment Program (RCAP) July 2013 and BCBS Analysis of risk-weighted assets for market-risk, RCAP, January and December 2013). While the BCBS was careful to attribute the differences mainly to factors such as differing supervisory guidance and the like, the findings dealt a serious blow to both supervisory and investor confidence in reported risk weights and led inexorably to closer scrutiny of the deviations between standardised and internal models and to the search for a formula which would limit abusive uses of the internal models without doing away with the idea of risk sensitivity. Both regulators and supervisors on the one hand and banks on the other hand were heavily invested in the idea. The banks of course had invested large sums of money in systems designed to measure risk sensitivity and had built up their risk management systems around this concept. But regulators and supervisors too were invested in this system and had built their own regulatory and supervisory systems around it. So no one was enthusiastic about a return to the "risk bucket" approach of Basel I.

The search led to a series of proposals, including (i) eliminating the use of internal models for certain kinds of risk which are viewed as not susceptible to modeling, such as operational risk, (ii) introducing input floors, which would prevent financial institutions from assuming "probability of default," "loss given default" and "exposure at default" on credit instruments below certain prescribed levels, for certain kinds of low default portfolios and (iii) most controversially introducing "output floors," limits below which RWAs calculated under internal models could not fall.

A caricature of a debate

While the proposals came from the experts on the staff of the BCBS, the search was often portrayed on the outside as no more than a regional dispute between the United States, very much in favor of limiting the use of internal models, and the European Union, very much invested in retaining them, against the backdrop of fundamental differences in the markets for financial services and important differences in overall approach to bank regulation. It was said that the United States is much less dependent on bank finance than Europe. This is true, bank finance there represents one-third versus two-thirds for market-based finance, with the percentages reversed in Europe. It was further said the U.S. banks did not really care about the Basel capital rules for several reasons. First, because the United States never adopted Basel II and therefore could not be relied upon to adopt Basel III. This was only partly true since Basel II did apply to all large, internationally active U.S. banks, but effective rhetoric, despite the fact that by 2013 the United States had, in fact, already adopted the first part of Basel III and, as Sandie O'Connor points out in her contribution to this volume, did so in a substantially more stringent manner than the form finally agreed to last December. Second, in the United States the binding constraints would in any event not be the Basel rules, but the leverage ratio, the Federal Reserve's CCAR stress tests and the Collins Amendment under the Dodd Frank Act which provides for a floor on setting risk-based capital for U.S. banks at effectively 100% of the standardised model, so that the U.S. banks would be indifferent to what was agreed in Basel. This again was only partly true, but sufficiently so to muddy the waters, especially for the non-experts.

Consequently, it was argued that the Europeans needed to hold on to the concept of RWAs and to find every way to reduce the calculation of risk capital because if they did not, their banks would face horrendously high requirements to raise additional capital in a market where capital was either unavailable or very expensive, while the Americans would face no such requirements. Consulting firms obligingly provided alarming estimates that "Basel IV" would increase RWAs by 40%–65%, resulting in capital shortfalls of 30%–50% and the need for as much as €7 trillion in additional capital for European banks. This dispute was taking place against a backdrop of economic recovery and perceived greater health of the banking sector in the United States versus continuing slow economic recovery in Europe and perceived problems with the European banks' balance sheets. Banks on both sides of the Atlantic were also quick to point out any and all possible negative effects on their ability to extend credit and other financial services as a result of increased regulation. In Europe this discussion focused particularly on any attempts to increase the effective need for capital of its banks through the tightening of the Basel III rules, using the slogan "Basel IV" to stigmatise the attempts to strengthen uniformity of results in measuring regulatory capital. This ultimately resulted in some European governments drawing a line in the sand that any regulatory changes could not result in a significant increase in capital requirements for their banks because that would hinder economic recovery. In a sense this reframed the discussion from one between a public good, financial stability and protecting taxpayers from having to pay for future bank failures, and a private cost, more capital for the banks, to one between two public goods, financial stability and protection of shareholders, versus economic recovery. While there was a dearth of reliable data that increased regulation was holding back growth and some credible data to the contrary, including work done by the staff of the Bank for International Settlements cited by Claudio Borio in his excellent contribution to this volume (see, e.g. Ingo Fender and Ulf Lewrick, Adding it all up: the macroeconomic impact of Basel III and outstanding reform issues, BIS Working Papers No. 591, November 2016), this reframing made the situation of the unelected central banks and other regulators involved in the Basel negotiations all the more difficult.

Where the broader problems lay

But I believe that, beyond the obvious geographic tug of war reported in the press, the real issues the parties were grappling with are what I have referred to as the regulatory trilemma. This concept is derived from the Mundell/Fleming trilemma in international economics, a theory which posits the incompatibility of fixed exchange rates, free capital movement and an independent monetary policy. This catchy phrase and the concept behind it have been applied to numerous other fields. Dani Rodrik famously adapted it to politics, positing the incompatibility of democracy, national sovereignty and global economic integration. And it has been repurposed to analyse Brexit as the outcome of the incompatibility of the single market, national sovereignty and democratic politics. This has led me to a somewhat less dramatic but nonetheless thorny trilemma – the difficulty in the area of financial regulation of reconciling three fundamental goals: risk sensitivity, comparability and simplicity. These are the three values the BCBS considered in designing the Basel III system. (Basel Committee on Banking Supervision, 2013, the regulatory framework balancing risk sensitivity, simplicity and comparability – discussion paper, http://www.bis.org/publ/bcbs258.pdf.).

A system lacking risk sensitivity will result in either too much or too little capital for the risks involved, leading either to inefficient allocation of societal resources or to dangers for the stability of the financial system. A system which lacks comparability will fail the fundamental goal of allowing both supervisors and investors to compare institutions, regulate them evenhandedly and price their securities accurately. Finally, a system which lacks simplicity will become a black box to those on the outside and an invitation to gaming the system to those on the inside, as well as a sinkhole for compliance and risk management spending, distracting attention from the forest of actual risk to the trees of reporting and compliance and thus failing the primary goal of allowing the proper assessment and management of risk. There is ample evidence that as systems become more complex, they generate the tendency to manage to rule rather than to manage risk. Each of these three is in itself an important goal for financial regulation, but together I suggest they constitute a trilemma, one corner of which had to give to achieve the best possible result. And how to achieve that, I propose, was the core element of the discussions which have occupied us for the last year, as a result of which I see significant gains in comparability and some gains in simplicity, admittedly at the cost of some sensitivity but, as we say in the US, "two out of three ain't bad."

The progression of complexity from Basel I through Basel II to Basel III, famously illustrated by Andy Haldane of the Bank of England in his speech and related paper on the dog and the frisbee, persuasively shows that complexity grows with risk sensitivity. As noted in the 2013 BCBS working paper, large internationally acting banks may have hundreds of models. And as systems become more complex they also become less robust when compared to simpler systems, also a theme Andy Haldane has mined to great effect. (Haldane, Andy and Vasileios Madaeros, The dog and the frisbee, Bank of England, 31 August 2012, accessed 31 March 2018). They also become rigid and goals in themselves. (See Goodhart's law on what happens when measures become targets). People tend to manage the output of the system which they no longer can master. By 2012 it was estimated that 90% of banks were using regulatory capital as their preferred capital metric in preference to the more traditional economic capital measure. (McKinsey & Company, Capital Management, Banking's new imperative, McKinsey Working Paper on Risk, Number 38, November 2012). So I think it was inevitable, once it became clear that this complexity was also leading to a lack of comparability, that complexity would have to give, because comparability is at the heart of the ability to regulate, supervise and invest effectively. Simplicity, in contrast, can be seen as a more abstract value, a "nice to have" feature, with a theoretical advantage of robustness, which participants in the debate considered, but not one as central to making the system work as comparability, and it was going up against the huge investments, sunk costs if you will, represented by the RWAs system for both the banks and their supervisors. The 2013 BCBS working paper explicitly recognises that simplicity has not been an explicit objective on a par with the two others, so I fear that it was also foreseeable that it would not come out on top, but only mildly improved.

Where we ended up

Those who think that risk sensitivity was sacrificed on the altar of agreement or, in my conceptual structure, of comparability and simplicity, are referred to the admirable contributions of Sabine Lautenschläger of the European Central Bank (ECB) and Mike Gibson of the Board of Governors of the Federal Reserve System to this volume. Sabine sets out with her accustomed great clarity where the freedom to use internal models was actually cut back: where they did not work, where either the bank had no better information than the supervisors or where there was no good basis for a model, as with operational risk. The addition of input floors and output floors put a collar on the deviations from the standardised model but in no way eliminated the idea of risk sensitivity. In fact, as Sabine points out, the standardised model has been made more risk sensitive precisely so it could better act as a fall back for an internal model that goes beyond the pale. This is an important point that has perhaps not gotten as much attention as it deserves. To allow the standardised model to serve as a more realistic fallback and frame of reference for internal models, Basel III has enhanced its risk sensitivity, moving it further away from the old "risk bucket" approach of Basel I. For example, residential mortgages under Basel II were largely assigned a single risk weight, reminiscent of Basel I's approach, but under Basel III, their risk weight will depend on their loan to value ratio, a clear gain in risk sensitivity. Also, as she points out and as I have noted above, banks have traditionally used the standardised approach for some parts of their assets, so these assets are effectively valued at 100%, giving those banks more leeway to value other assets at less than the 72.5% level they must meet overall by 2027.

Mike Gibson notes that despite hopes that complexity could be reduced by the final agreement, in fact the complex internal risk calculations remain, and they remain complex. I still think some progress has been made, as does Mike, though more would have been desirable. But international accords on banking standards turn out to be, like politics, the art of the possible.

One point on which I respectfully disagree with many of the speakers during the course of the day and as reflected in some of their contributions to this volume is the suggestion that the 10 year phase-in period for the banks to fully implement the output floors, starting at 50% in January 2022 and ending at 72.5% in

January 2027, means they do not have to concern themselves with an immediate need to raise capital and can clearly earn their way out of any risk-weighted capital deficit over those 10 years. I think this hope is undercut by what happened with the initial Basel III rules (the numerator phase) when every analyst immediately asked to see "fully loaded" numbers as of the end of the phase-in period right away, thus putting immediate pressure on the banks involved to do something about their capital deficits. I agree that there is a difference here. As Stuart Graham notes in his contribution to the volume, until the banks are required to publish their new standardised RWAs, it is extremely difficult to calculate the gap from outside. This should build in a bit of a time buffer. However, as Stuart also points out, as soon as those numbers are published, and he puts the most likely date at 2021, so well before 2027, frontloading is very likely to occur. On the other hand, referring to the European Banking Authority's (EBA) ad hoc cumulative impact assessment of the Basel III final package cited by Sabine and Andreas Dombret in their contributions to this volume, I would note that the estimated shortfalls were calculated on the basis of bank balance sheets as of December 2015, not taking into account capital raised since then and the EBA's estimate of €34.4 billion seems rather modest compared to the alarmist estimates of €7 trillion floated by consultants a year earlier. Stuart also concludes that European banks will not need to raise equity to meet the new standards and that only a handful will have to reduce expected payouts to reach them.

This is not to say that the transition will be painless for banks across the board. It is clear from the discussion of the geographical impact of Basel III at the conference and in this volume that European banks are likely to be most affected. But it is important to note that the size of the impact is related to the starting point for the institutions involved. Banks which have been reporting RWAs on the order of one-third of their balance sheet total and banks carrying large amounts of non-performing loans on their books are of course starting further back in the pack than banks reporting RWAs closer to the 60% of their balance sheet assets and who have been forced by market and regulatory and supervisory pressure to clean up their balance sheets.

What remains to be done

1. Sovereign debt risk weights

Two main issues remain after the December 7, 2017 agreement, one issue on which no consensus could be reached, the risk weight of sovereign debt, and implementation of the agreement. The risk weight of sovereign debt is a particular problem for the European Union. The initial decision to grant a zero risk weight to sovereign debt issued in the currency of the sovereign for banks incorporated in the jurisdiction of the sovereign was based on the idea that in a world of fiat money, a sovereign could always avoid default of instruments issued in its own currency since it could always issue more of that currency to meet its debt obligations. The European Union extended this principle to any debt issued in Euros by a Member State of the EU. But no Member State can issue Euros to cover its debt, only the European Central Bank can do so, so the risk of default by an over-indebted Member State cannot be excluded. As I have written before in a previous volume in this ILF Series, an EU Member State issuing debt in Euros is closer to an emerging markets state issuing debt in US dollars than to Japan issuing debt in Yen.

This was the crux or, better, the driving engine of the euro-zone financial crisis in 2010–2012, better known as the vicious circle between banks and sovereigns and was one motor for the European Union's Banking Union project. The particular problem is two-fold. First, if EU Member State sovereign debt were weighted according to their ratings by credit rating agencies, fewer than half would earn a zero risk weight, with the balance having risk weights of 20% or 50%, or in the case of one outlier at 100%. Second, much of this debt tends to be concentrated in the hands of domestic financial institutions, who have with some accuracy been labeled the buyers of last resort for their sovereigns' debt. As such, they can play an important stabilising role in panic selling situations, albeit at a potential risk to the institutions involved. So no sovereign can be expected to welcome changes which could interfere with this function. It should also be noted that under the liquidity requirements of Basel III and for purposes of borrowing from central banks, where it serves as eligible collateral, holding of liquid government debt is in any event implicitly encouraged, so these holdings should not be expected to evaporate.

Thus, what risk weight to assign is clearly a highly political question which has led to disagreement among the Member States. Ways around this political dilemma, such as limiting the amount of sovereign debt exposure individual financial institutions may hold, are possible alternatives to assigning a more than zero weight, but it is to be feared that progress will be slow on this front.

2. But the devil is in the implementation

The same may well apply to overall implementation of Basel III in the European Union. The next European Parliament elections are scheduled for May 2019, as Martin Merlin notes in his contribution to this volume, and the current Commission is only aiming to table a legislative proposal on Basel III sometime in 2020 and that only after a public consultation on the matter. While public consultations always sound like good ideas, to hold one after this long drawn-out process smacks a bit of a second (or twenty-second) bite at the apple. If Christian Ossig's extremely interesting contribution to this volume is any evidence, that consultation could bring forth a number of new proposals on how to implement these standards. The record of the Commission implementing prior rounds of Basel III has not always been exemplary. As Claudio Borio notes in his excellent contribution to this volume, EU implementation has in the past been graded "materially non-compliant" by the Basel Committee and we know that much of the foot-dragging on the current agreement came from European quarters. So until Europe shows its cards in 2020, I fear other partners may be disinclined to hasten to implement the agreement to the letter. I thus agree entirely with Andreas Dombret's call in his contribution to this volume for the Commission not to delay implementation.

Beyond the usual attempts to retrade lost points in the course of implementation, which were a feature of the negotiation of the Fourth Capital Markets Directive (CRD IV) where elements explicitly excluded from the numerator of bank capital in the first round of Basel III were nonetheless restored for European banks in CRD IV and minimums were turned into maximums, there is an additional issue for European Union implementation this time. It is the issue Andreas Dombret refers to as "proportionality." As Martin Merlin of the European Commission staff notes in his contribution to this volume, the EU "contrary to most other jurisdictions" has so far opted to apply the Basel rules, initially designed only for internationally active banks, in their entirety to all banks in their jurisdiction. This is somewhat of an overbroad statement, as can be seen by the detailed analysis contained in the Financial Stability Institute's FSI Insights on policy implementation No. 1, Proportionality in banking regulation: a cross-country comparison, Bank for International Settlements, August 2017, which notes elements of proportionality within the implementation of the Basel rules within the EU.

However, as the rules have become ever more complex, the compliance burden for smaller banks has grown disproportionately and it is appropriate to pay additional attention to the issue of disproportionate compliance burdens on small- and medium-sized banks. Jurisdictions as diverse as Brazil, the Hong Kong SAR, Japan, Switzerland and the United States have opted to apply Basel rules in full only to a subset of their banks. The case of Brazil could be particularly interesting to the European Union in that it had initially opted to apply Basel II and II.5 to all 1,400 of its financial institutions, but with Basel III, has changed its approach towards greater proportionality. As the FSI Insights paper notes, the urge to apply proportionality is greatest in jurisdictions such as Brazil, Switzerland and the United States where there are a large number of small banks whose business model, range of activities and lack of international activities make them particularly unlikely to endanger financial stability at home or to upset the "level playing field" internationally and that where the line is drawn on reporting or other relief usually results in 70% or more of the banking assets in the jurisdiction being subject to the full Basel III set of rules and, in the United States, to additional, more stringent rules as well.

Andreas Dombret, in his contribution to this volume, makes an excellent case for a broader use of proportionality in the implementation of Basel III and it is clear that given the number of small- and medium-sized (or, in the parlance of the Single Supervisory Mechanism, "less significant") banks in Germany and Austria as compared to most other EU countries, the issue is particularly important to those two countries, in contrast to the much more centralised banking systems in other EU Member States, such as the Netherlands, Greece or Finland, so whether Andreas' excellent arguments will find sufficient support within the European Union remains to be seen even though I believe the logic of his arguments is compelling. The idea is not to relieve small- and medium-sized institutions from substantive rules of Basel III, but rather from some of the detailed compliance burdens. If proportionality were implemented in a reasonable fashion, many of the complaints about the complexity of Basel III would be dealt with at a stroke. To refuse proportionality based on a decision to apply the rules more broadly than elsewhere seems to handicap the European Union's banking system to no great profit.

One thing, however, is clear. Until the December 7, 2017 agreement has been implemented, the full benefits of the certainty which the accord was meant to bring to all stakeholders, financial institutions, their investors, supervisors and regulators will probably not be realised in full, so that holding back on implementation simply contributes to deferring further the already long deferred benefits of the accord. The devil, as we all know, is in the details and there is much detailed work yet to do – so, only in the broadest sense can we say we are done now.

IV: **But have we gone far enough?**

C.A.E. Goodhart, Financial Markets Group,
London School of Economics

Have the regulatory authorities done enough?

Introduction

The critical academic literature on capital adequacy requirements (CARs) has mostly focussed on whether these required ratios are high enough, see for example Miles, et al. (2012) and Admati and Hellwig (2013); in recent years, this has been accompanied by discussion of whether bail-inable bonds and contingent convertible bonds (Co-Co) can act in some part as substitutes for equity within total loss absorbing capital (TLAC) and its close cousin minimum requirement for own funds and eligible liabilities (MREL). Partly because so much careful attention has already been given to this issue, not least in the associated Chapter by Prof. Schnabel, with whom I shared the conference session on this subject, I shall herewith bypass these issues. Instead, I discuss four wider matters relating to the work of the Basel Committee on Banking Supervision (BCBS). I shall argue that there are several facets of regulation to which the authorities have not given sufficient attention.

But before I start on this, I want to make a general comment. I would like to reiterate the general expression at this conference that the BCBS has achieved some remarkable and highly beneficial reforms. All that Stefan Ingves stated in his opening presentation about these achievements is indeed correct. Moreover, one should acknowledge the importance of central bankers and others working together at the BCBS in achieving a compromise overall agreement to complete Basel III, at a time when there are quite severe centrifugal forces tending to dismantle the international monetary and trading systems. Such a compromise general agreement shows that central bankers at least are prepared to stand together and reach international agreements for the benefit of all, even when some of the rough edges are not to the best liking of their own national banking systems; a very considerable achievement.

But financial regulation is procyclical

However, as an opening critical comment, the conduct and comments at this conference have reinforced my view that financial regulation, like almost every other

https://doi.org/10.1515/9783110621495-009

aspect of finance, is procyclical. After a crisis, the cry goes up, quite properly, "That must never be allowed to happen again." Consequently, regulation after a crisis gets tightened, often severely. But this is just at a time when commercial bankers, and others in finance, are themselves most risk adverse, with sizeable loan losses, low profitability and weak markets. Thus, after such a crisis, commercial bankers are already drawing in their horns, and tending to be less expansionary, even contracting. On top of this, the tightened regulations are likely to involve further headwinds restricting credit expansion. It is, of course, true that in such circumstances those banks with higher and better capital ratios will be lending more. But it is an error to believe that that implies that an enforced regulatory transition for the banks to higher capital ratios will lead to more lending; rather the reverse will happen unless the transition is handled with great skill and care. How far the transition from much lower regulatory ratios to higher ones enhanced in recent years the headwinds against financial expansion, or not, is a difficult issue to resolve, and would require some careful empirical work, which would take the discussion wider than there is time or, in my case, the ability to undertake here.

But what I do want to emphasise is that as the recovery does eventually come through, in large part because of the successful actions of the central banks themselves, the factors making bankers more cautious and risk averse will also erode and reverse. Banking profits will rise, loan losses decline, equity markets recover and animal spirits get refreshed. Partly because everything seems to be going well, the cry then becomes that the prior tightening of financial regulation has gone far enough, or even too far, and needs to be clawed back in part. But it is in exactly such good times, as Minsky described, that the worst risks get taken on, largely because, during good times, these do not appear to be risks at all.

In such cases there is a tendency for regulation to be loosened, with a move towards light-touch regulation, based on general principles, just at a time when financial expansion and actual risk-seeking is increasing. While the tough times involve tightened regulation, the good times generally have easier regulation.

The presentations at this conference lead me to be fairly sure that we are currently at an inflection point, a dividing line, between the tough regulatory times and the good times when regulation ceases to keep up with risk adoption. The very title of the conference, whether we have done enough, now that Basel III is completed and the comments about regulatory sabbaticals, all lead me to be pretty sure that this conference marks just such a dividing line. Whereas for much of the last 8 years or so, much of my own policy advice has been that the regulators need to be more careful that the tightened regulations should not add to the headwinds holding back bank credit expansion, now I think that the situation has changed. Academics like me need to be much more concerned that the desideratum will be to prevent regulators from allowing the financial system to become ever more exposed to risk in the context of good times, and a generalised economic boom.

Regulation is designed in silos, not holistically

Within the field of liquidity requirements we now have two separate ratios for banks to maintain, LCR, the liquidity coverage ratio, and the NSFR, the net stable funding ratio. Yet these two are closely interconnected, as Cecchetti and Schoenholtz (2017) have demonstrated. Do we need both? Could not the better designed moving parts of both be reformulated into a single ratio?

Similarly, within the field of capital requirements, there are two alternative techniques, the BCBS' CARs, with their various add-ons, such as the CCYB, the Counter Cyclical Buffer, and (a variety of) stress tests. What is the analytical relationship between these, or is it just a case of wanting belts and braces at a time of some uncertainty about the efficacy of either on their own? Theoretically those risks whose stochastic probability distribution is known should be met by the application of appropriate risk spreads. Instead capital should be held to protect against relatively rare, and largely unforecastable in timing, tail risks. But that would seem to imply, prima facie, that stress tests should become the main fulcrum for the application of capital ratios, not the Basel III CARs. But I heard little, or nothing, at the conference about the interaction between stress tests and CARs. Perhaps I missed it, as I had to leave early.

Similarly liquidity and capital requirements are usually discussed independently of each other, when they should not be. A financial institution with little, or no, maturity mismatch and plentiful liquid assets needs less protective capital. The more the liquid, the less need for capital. When I was young in the 1960s, and earlier, there were quite restrictive required liquidity ratios, but no required capital ratios. Then that got reversed in the 1980s. Was that switch good, or bad? Now that we have requirements for both capital and liquidity, what should be their relationship? Is it satisfactory to treat them in isolation?

In a sense, but only up to a point, the risk weights applied to the various assets in the calculation of risk-weighted assets (RWAs) have in some cases a connection to liquidity, but the very low weight applied to residential mortgages, especially in some internal risk-based (IRB) models is a counterexample. As with the case of stress tests, I heard virtually no discussion of the relationship between liquidity and capital at the conference, but perhaps I missed something.

There is a story, possibly apocryphal, that a banker, reputed to be Jamie Dimon, once asked Ben Bernanke, when Ben was Chairman of the Fed, whether anyone had ever calculated the overall, aggregate effect of *all* the proposed regulations simultaneously on the banks. The answer apparently was "no." The nub of the criticism here is that bank regulators are too inclined to design such regulations in mental silos, whereas the regulations actually have an interactive effect on the banks and other financial institutions to which they apply. Trying to approach financial regulation holistically is, no doubt, difficult. If it was easy it would have been done. My concern is that I see little evidence of regulators trying to approach these issues holistically. Where, for example, do the regulators spell out the best way for liquidity and capital requirements to interact? But perhaps I am failing to keep up with the relevant literature.

Apply regulation to bankers, rather than just to banks

Let me turn next to the third area where I think that the thrust of regulation, post the Great Financial Crisis (GFC), has been unbalanced. Such regulation has focussed almost entirely on applying requirements to banks, for example, in the form of CARs and LCR and NSFRs, rather than trying to bring about direct adjustments to bankers' incentives.

The key point is that a bank, although a legal person, is not a person but an inanimate institution. A bank can have no feeling, take no decisions, have no risk aversion and have no strategies. All these feelings, decisions, attitudes to risk and strategies are actually undertaken by human bankers, not by inanimate banks.

Let me take what is perhaps the most egregious example where putting the focus on banks rather than on bankers is far from the best way of proceeding. This is particularly the case when fining banks for the bad behaviour undertaken by individual bankers. If I may take a football analogy, it is roughly the equivalent of having the referee penalise fouls conducted on the playing field by the players (bankers) by requiring the fans in the stands (shareholders) to pay, each of them a large financial penalty in order to go on watching the game. This does have some indirect beneficial effect, in that the fans (shareholders) would lobby the owners[1] and managers to impose tougher codes of conduct and good behaviour on their players (junior bank managers). But it is unethical, because it penalises those innocent of any wrongdoing. It is macroeconomically inefficient, because the very considerable loss of bank capital involved has represented yet another

1 In the United Kingdom most of the leading clubs have very concentrated ownership.

major headwind during the tough times from which we are just emerging. It is inefficient because it is indirect; moreover, by the time that the fines eventually become levied, both the managers and the players involved have frequently moved on to other roles. Altogether the process of fining banks for bankers' misdeeds has been a spectacular own goal.

But even more important, there has been insufficient realisation of the moral hazard involved in enabling those involved in taking the key decisions that influence bank outcomes to enjoy limited liability on their shareholdings. If I may adapt a Biblical phrase, too many economists and commentators strain at the moral hazard gnat of deposit insurance, while swallowing whole the moral hazard camel of limited liability for bank managers, directors and controlling shareholders. A recent book which sets out these points very nicely is by Kokkinis on *Corporate Law and Financial Instability*, (2018), which I recommend.

With bank managers having an incentive to maximise return on equity (ROE) and short-term equity prices, there is always going to be an inbuilt problem in designing CARs. If the risk weights are going to be set by the regulators, there are always bound to be distortions of the regulatory weights relative to the perceived economic risks, as in Basel I. Recall that a camel was a horse constructed by a committee, and the problems get worse when such a committee gets influenced by political considerations. On the other hand, if the risk weights are set by bank modellers, on some internal model basis, so long as bank managers have the current incentives, such weights are bound to be gamed and manipulated, as in Basel II. The book by Bayoumi, *Unfinished Business*, blames much of the GFC on this basis.

The best resolution of banking crises in recent times was that done in Scandinavia in the early 1990s, quite largely through the excellent work of Stefan Ingves. That was done by a bail-out and temporary nationalisation, which was effective then.[2] But that mechanism now has been rejected largely because of political outcry. But that outcry was not because people wanted to see their banks close and go into liquidation, but because bankers appeared to get away scot-free. Virtually all the senior bankers involved left in circumstances which allowed them to live a life of wealth and comfort after the event. Fred Goodwin and Dick Fuld are two examples in point. If we are to get the public onside, from a political

2 Partly because nationalisation is such a politically-charged action, it was done on some occasions during the 2008/9 crisis in ways that reflected political, rather than economic, priorities. Thus the Labour government injected capital into the Royal Bank of Scotland rather than fully nationalising it. It is arguable that nationalisation, and wiping out all the shareholders and imposing a charge on (some of) the junior creditors, would have been a cleaner procedure, and have prevented the drawn-out continuation of the UK government's involvement in RBS, and the resulting complexity about managerial objectives.

economy viewpoint, it will be necessary for them to feel that the punishment has fitted the crime. Could we ever get to the point where the penalty on bankers who have led the system into crisis would be so severe that the public actually feels sorry for them, as the public felt sorry for shareholders after the City of Glasgow bank failure in 1878? While it is good that bail-in (TLAC and MREL) shift some of the costs of failure onto private sector junior creditors, what is really needed is to shift much more of the costs onto the bankers themselves.

There have been some moves in that direction, perhaps particularly in the United Kingdom. This has involved the possibility of clawback of unvested bonuses, the new Senior Managers Regime and the possibility of charging bankers with reckless banking. But, as Kokkinis' book sets out nicely, it is highly unlikely that any of these will really have a major effect of changing the incentive structure of bankers and financiers more generally.

One of the common slogans "No banker got sent to jail" is attributed to Alan Greenspan. But one should be more careful. Bankers have been sent to jail, but mostly for conduct of business crimes, involving fraud, contagious price fixing, etc. The point of the complaint, instead, is that no one in senior management who took the risky actions, for example, massive increases in leverage that landed the financial system into such a severe crisis, ever seemed to suffer severely from the resulting failure. But the criminal law, and jail sentences, are not, on this view, the answer; Goodwin and Fuld neither wanted, nor expected, their banks to collapse. There was no *mens rea*. The better route is to adjust the law to allow a greater possibility of civil suit and financial penalties, as discussed further below.

On this view, much more could and should be done. Perhaps the most promising route would be to open up bankers to civil suit; the criminal law is inappropriate in most such cases, because there is often no intention to harm, and even when there is *mens rea*, it is often extraordinarily difficult to prove in a court of law. Furthermore, the bankers involved would have to be prevented from taking out insurance to protect themselves from the fines that might be imposed under civil suit judgements. My own preference would be to abrogate the ability of senior managers to protect themselves through limited liability. For example, a CEO might be required to have unlimited liability, whereas senior managers below him might be required to have multiple liability.[3] Again, it might be possible to require the payment of all bonuses to take the form of bail-inable bonds. If the remuner-

3 But what about the traders, and others, taking risks, and in some cases acting illegally, at more junior levels? They are less likely to have many shares. In this case, a better approach is to make their manager(s) open to civil suit for failing to control their subordinates. The traders, taking the excessive risks, would have more upside benefit, than their managers. So if there was downside risk to the manager, she would be given a clear incentive to be more watchful. The New Zealand

ation of senior managers took such a form, it would be my view that banks would swiftly move to much higher equity ratios to protect the value of their bonuses. In discussion this was challenged by our moderator, Doug Elliott, who argued that the ability of ordinary shareholders, who would retain limited liability, to appoint or dismiss bank management would mean that the emphasis on ROE and short-term equity price maximisation would remain. Certainly the tension between the objectives of shareholders seeking short-term profit maximisation and managers paid largely in bail-inable bonds would be creative, and, in my view, lead to a better balance between the objectives of society as a whole and those of shareholders.

It is, in my view, arguable that the managers of any limited liability company should have incentives to care for other stakeholders and for society as a whole, rather than just have their incentives aligned to those of their shareholders, for reasons set out by Smithers (2013). But the case for doing so is much stronger in the case of banks, where shareholder equity is typically such a small percentage of their funding and the effect on the economy of contagious failure is so much greater than in most other industries.

The structure of housing finance

I was glad to learn during the course of the conference that one of the effects of the Basel III compromise was to raise the risk weights applied to housing finance in specialised mortgage banks, and other banks focussing primarily on housing finance. While this is a move in the right direction, again I do not think that this has gone anything like far enough.

As Schularick and Taylor have demonstrated in several articles, together with various other co-authors, the basis of most crises in the last few decades has been that banks have undertaken long-term illiquid mortgage-based property finance on the basis, quite largely, of short-term wholesale funding provided by informed, but uninsured, lenders. When things go wrong in such real estate markets, this is a recipe for disaster. However, during the good times, which cover most years, the failures and loan losses involved in such finance tend to be much smaller than for most other private sector lending. I recall one example of risk weighting based on historical experience involving two banks, one of which had been undertaking mortgage lending during the crisis of 1991/2 in the United Kingdom, while the other had only gone into such mortgage lending in subsequent years. The

approach of requiring Directors to sign an affidavit that they had each examined internal control mechanisms and were content that they were adequate could be broadened.

risk weights that they applied differed by a factor of almost ten, since the bank that had taken up mortgage lending after that crisis had no experience of significant loan losses in the United Kingdom thereafter. Banks in countries which have avoided such crises will put forward models involving minimal credit risks from housing finance. Similarly, on a backwards-looking basis, in the autumn of 2007, the experience of loan losses in Northern Rock of mortgage financing was negligibly small, whereas looking forward to the much more difficult market of 2008 and subsequently, many investors thought, in the event quite rightly, that it was insolvent. Thus the risk weights that bankers will claim appropriate will often largely depend purely on whether there has been a major crisis in the housing market in recent history, that is, in the last 20 years, or so. But such housing crises can occur anywhere. Forward-looking stress tests can help diminish such problems.

If the NSFR is to achieve its purpose, it should encourage a shift of funding of such mortgage lending from short-term forms to equivalent long-term funding, such for example as the Danish Covered Bond mechanism. Insofar as the narrow banking enthusiasts are serious, they ought to start with housing finance, requiring such long-term illiquid lending to be matched by similarly long-term funding, because that is where both maturity mismatch and systemic risk has been worst.

But I see no signs of that happening, no doubt because of political sensitivities. Indeed, I see no real tendency to grasp the nettle of the unbalanced structure of housing finance. To take but one example of the stasis in this field, the problems in the United States with the form and structure of Fannie Mae and Freddie Mac have not moved forward one inch. This remains the soft underbelly of systemic risk, and no one seems willing to tackle it.

Bibliography

Admati, A., and M. Hellwig, (2013), *The Bankers' New Clothes: What's Wrong with Banking and What to Do about It*', Princeton University Press.

Bayoumi, T., (2017), *Unfinished Business: The Unexplored Causes of the Financial Crisis and the Lessons Yet to be Learned*, Yale University Press.

Cecchetti, S.G., and K. Schoenholtz, (2017), "Regulatory Reform: A Scorecard," Centre for Economic Policy Research Discussion Paper DP12465, November.

Kokkinis, A., (2018), *Corporate Law and Financial Instability*, Routledge.

Miles, D., Yang, J., and G. Marcheggiano, (2012), "Optimal Bank Capital," *The Economic Journal*, Volume 123, Issue 567, March, pp 1–37.

Smithers, A., (2013), *The Road to Recovery: How and Why Economic Policy Must Change*, John Wiley & Sons.

Isabel Schnabel, Professor, Bonn University, and
Member of the German Council of Economic Experts

But have we gone far enough?

At the conference we have heard a lot of praise for the achievements through the conclusion of the Basel III negotiations, and, of course, the long-awaited end to the negotiations was indeed a relief for many, including academics like Charles Goodhart and myself. "But have we gone far enough?" – the question we were asked to address suggests that one may have wished for more.

Is Basel III a success?

Overall, I think it is fair to say that Basel III is a big step forward. The quality of bank capital was improved, the level of capital requirements was raised, new macroprudential instruments were defined, a minimum leverage ratio was specified and a liquidity regulation was introduced in order to limit banks' liquidity and maturity transformation. All these were crucial steps, but they were all part of the initial negotiations, concluded still under the fresh impression of the global financial crisis.

The second phase of the Basel III negotiations led to results that are much more technical and much harder to understand for non-experts. One of the main parameters of the negotiations had been more or less fixed in advance: It had been agreed that this second round should not increase aggregate capital requirements for banks significantly. Although it is open to debate what this meant precisely, this agreement limited the scope of the potential outcomes of the negotiations before they had even started. It had not been preceded by any analysis showing convincingly that capital levels were now high enough to make the global financial system stable. It was the outcome of a political process and a reflection of the fact that the crisis was already too long ago to be remembered for what it was: one of the most severe disruptions of the global financial system ever.

The agreement was also a success for banking lobbies worldwide, which had succeeded in convincing central banks, supervisors and politicians equally that higher capital would be harmful, that it would choke the incipient recovery and that it would lead to a harmful credit crunch in economies starving for loans. According to the estimations by the European Banking Authority, the second phase of the Basel III negotiations will raise aggregate capital requirements by

https://doi.org/10.1515/9783110621495-010

very little, much less than the changes in the first phase.[1] Almost half of this amount concerns European banks, which is largely a reflection of a laxer regulation before.

Given that aggregate capital was not supposed to rise overall to any significant extent, the negotiations amounted to a reshuffling of requirements, raising them for some banks but lowering them for others. In the end, they were raised mainly for larger banks following the internal ratings-based approach (but probably less than had been feared) and lowered for smaller ones using the standardised approach.

Besides the add-on on the leverage ratio requirement for globally significant institutions, the most important change is the introduction of an output floor, which limits the scope of banks using the internal ratings-based approach to credit measurement ("IRB banks") to reduce their requirements below the outcome of the standardised approach, while not changing the general, risk-based approach to regulation. The settlement on 72.5% looks like a sensible compromise between the involved negotiating parties, which had been stuck between 70% and 75%. However, this number, which was publicised widely in the press, is not informative without seeing it jointly with the base to which it is linked, namely the outcome of the standardised approach. In fact, the alleviations of the standardised approach are benefiting not only the smaller banks using this approach but also indirectly the IRB banks through the output floor. Moreover, IRB banks are benefitting from the removal of the scaling factor of 1.06. The overly long transition phases, including those for the Fundamental Review of the Trading Book, were another concession made to the banks, and so it did not come as a surprise that stocks markets reacted very positively to the outcomes of the negotiations.

Regarding the regulatory trilemma, stressed by Patrick Kenadjian, in his contributions to this volume, it seems to me that the goal of maintaining risk sensitivity and furthering comparability across banks could be achieved only by giving in further on simplicity.

Rising complexity

Even experts find it difficult to predict the precise implications that the agreement will have for bank capital. One certain outcome of the negotiations is that regulation is becoming even more complex. This complexity partly reflects the

1 European Banking Authority, Ad hoc cumulative impact assessment of the Basel reform package, 20 December 2017.

lobbying activities of various countries, which seem to have followed the motto "national banks' competitiveness first" rather than "systemic stability first." Some parts of Basel III read like a wish list of various countries, like the "hard test" for mortgage loans, which seems to be tailor-made for German banks. Such rules are also not always consistent with the alleged wish to foster risk sensitivity, as is, for example, the case with loan splitting. Many of these concessions have, in fact, gone rather unnoticed in the general public.

Right after the conclusion of the negotiations, the lobbying continued. Banking associations talked immediately about the need for adjusting the regulation to national specificities and for a proportionality for smaller banks, where "small" often includes a large spectrum of banks. The European Commission already promised to hold a consultation and impact assessment in order to evaluate the consequences for the EU economy before transposing the agreement into EU law. There is, hence, large uncertainty about the transposition of the Basel agreement in national law in the EU and elsewhere, and there is clearly the danger of significant dilutions. The Commission should withstand the temptation to make further concessions to European banks and should not allow that the legitimate demand for proportionality leads to a dilution of prudential standards for smaller banks. Instead, they should raise the efficiency of regulation and consider expanding useful rules, such as the buffer on the leverage ratio for globally significant banks, to other significant institutions in Europe. This would also send a strong signal across the world to not dilute the rules agreed upon.

Is capital high enough?

The optimal level of bank capital from a system perspective is, of course, subject to debate. It is noteworthy, however, that most existing studies yield higher optimal capital ratios than the ones agreed upon, in particular with respect to the non-risk-weighted capital ratio. At the same time, very few papers confirm the alleged negative effects of higher capital on bank lending. If anything, the crisis has shown that countries with better capitalised banks were able to weather the crisis much better. One major reason is that low capital makes it much harder to deal with non-performing loans. High NPLs, in turn, can inhibit the lending to profitable firms, while promoting the development of a zombie economy.

The new regulatory approach builds on a combination of equity capital and bail-inable debt. However, as recent events in Italy have shown, a bail-in is politically difficult even in relatively calm times. Hence, it is even less likely that bail-in would fully work in a systemic crisis. At the same time, the rise in public debt makes it questionable whether states would be in the position to bail out banks as they did in 2008, which could give rise to instability. While a buffer of bail-inable debt is useful, it cannot replace appropriate levels of capital.

What is still missing?

In my view we are still in a position where the benefit of a further increase in the required capital would exceed the costs. More specifically, I am critical about the alleviations for mortgage loans as well as corporate loans. I am also struggling with the alleged benefits of an internal ratings-based approach. I haven't seen much evidence that the higher risk sensitivity leads to a better risk management, while there exists, for example, an interesting academic study by Markus Behn, Rainer Haselmann and Vikrant Vig claiming the opposite: default probabilities are systematically underestimated under an IRB approach and loans under the internal ratings-based approach had not only lower risk weights but also higher default probabilities (which were, in fact, reflected in higher interest rates).[2] I liked Stefan Ingves' analogy of an IRB approach being like "grading one's own exam." But it is even worse than that: When overstating the grade, this is not just unfair and generates a competitive advantage. It has – in the case of internal models – a negative impact on the class' overall performance, something that is, however, not taken into account by the student. The presence of such externalities is a severe conceptual problem of the IRB approach.

One unfortunate, though expected outcome is the lack of agreement on a proper regulation of sovereign exposures, which would have been crucial in order to break the nexus between sovereigns and banks. I think this debate is of utmost importance for global financial stability, and it should therefore be promoted not only in the euro area but also globally.

And I still believe that the interest rate risk in the banking book, which was not part of these negotiations, should be moved to Pillar 1, in order to ensure equal and high standards across banks and countries. In fact, this risk may be one of the major risks to be faced by banks in the years to come, when more and more central banks are going to tighten monetary policy.

---

2 Markus Behn, Haselmann, Rainer and Vig, Vikrant, The limits of model-based regulation, European Central Bank Working Paper Series No. 1928/July 2016.

Conclusion

Overall, I would conclude that we have made a big step forward with Basel III. But I would not yet be confident that we have gone far enough to be able to cope with the next big crisis. Capital levels are still too low, and I would not count too much on macroprudential regulation, which is still untested, and on the bail-in framework, which still shows some significant gaps. So maybe starting to think about Basel IV would not be such a bad idea after all?

Of course, this may be politically naive, or a "waste of time" as Andreas Dombret puts it. There is no appetite to think about further regulation at this moment. But as Stefan Ingves stressed in his keynote, at the very least, an evaluation process of the new regulations should be promoted following scientific standards. And if risks become apparent that have not been taken into account sufficiently, regulation should not wait until the next crisis for further reforms.

Douglas J. Elliott, Partner, Oliver Wyman

Did the Basel reforms go "Far Enough"?

The question posed to my panel was whether the Basel capital and liquidity reforms went "far enough." This is a very difficult question to answer analytically, despite its seeming simplicity. Effectively answering it requires focusing on a series of sub-questions. Before going into the details, the short version of my views is that the Basel standards put us broadly in the right range of aggregate levels of capital, based on many analyses from academics and official institutions. (There is no similar analytical basis for judging the liquidity standards, as far less academic work has been done on quantitative liquidity standards.) At the same time, there are legitimate concerns about many of the specifics, which do matter. So, my view is that the Basel standards are a big step forward, but leave considerable room for improvement. Now, on to those detailed questions:

First, do financial regulations, or at least those set up by the Basel Committee, even fit on a scale or a spectrum or is this concept misleading?

"Far enough" implies directionality after all. Parts of the reforms do fit neatly onto a scale, such as the minimum required level of tier 1 capital as a percentage of risk-weighted assets. One can argue about whether 8% is better than 4%, but we can at least agree that 8 is twice as big as 4. A second portion of the Basel reforms fit onto a scale, but less neatly. Changes in the definition of what instruments qualify as tier 1 capital, for example, force us to find a way to convert figures under the old definitions into equivalents under the new if we want to compare apples and near-apples. Assuming the conversion calculations are reasonably accurate in the aggregate, analysts can still compare old with new using a scale.

However, there are also important parts of the Basel reforms that simply cannot reliably be put onto a scale. There are many new or toughened procedural requirements, such as the substantially greater restrictions on the use of internal models to determine risk weights. It is a very complex and often quite subjective task to try to convert one's view of these procedural changes into an aggregate effect on total capital or other measures that can be compared on a scale.

Further, how should one view changes that have differential impacts within the industry? It is well accepted that the final round of reforms, what the industry refers to as "Basel IV," has substantially greater impact on European banks in the aggregate than on US banks. How "far" should we view these latest reforms as taking us? A big distance, based on effects in Europe, or hardly any distance at all, based on American impacts? There are similar issues within a given region or

https://doi.org/10.1515/9783110621495-011

country, depending on business models. A few banks likely had decreases in their capital requirements from the final round of changes, even though the aggregate effect on the industry was clearly an increase.

Then there are the difficult questions of the interactions between requirements and the impacts of second-order and dynamic effects. There are those who argue that forcing banks towards a system of capital requirements that are less risk-sensitive than in the past will lead to a rise in risk taking. In the extreme of this view, seemingly tougher requirements would lead to riskier banks and a riskier system. So, adding toughness could move the system farther from safety.

That all said, I do believe that it is meaningful and useful to analyse the aggregate impact of the Basel reforms on total capital levels for the industry as compared to Basel II. This is particularly true since the total effects are large. But, one must keep in mind the complications and caveats just outlined and not over-interpret the importance of the parts that can be more easily quantified, at the expense of recognising the other factors.

Second, if a scale is meaningful, what is measured on the scale, what would be the optimum point and where will we be after the Basel reforms fully kick in?

This enters into the realm of cost-benefit analysis. As someone who has written extensively on the costs and benefits of the Basel capital requirements – at The Brookings Institution, the IMF, and at Oliver Wyman – I do have views on this. However, it is important once again to add several caveats to any such analysis.

Caveat 1: We're still largely operating on theory, as it has been extremely difficult to measure the costs and benefits empirically. Despite the long history of capital requirements, and some pretty solid theory about them, we did not have much good empirical analysis even before the Global Financial Crisis. Post-crisis, empirical analysis of the reforms is hindered by a combination of the following: the inherent complexity; the massive number of moving parts given the huge changes in the economy, finance and regulation post-crisis; and the fact that regulatory changes are still being phased in. I hope that clever economists will find some natural experiments or other techniques to dig out the actual impacts soon. In the meantime, we continue to argue primarily based on long-standing theories.

Caveat 2: Existing theories generally rely either on fairly simplistic accounting frameworks or massively complex Dynamic General Stochastic Equilibrium (DGSE) models, in both cases making it difficult to have full confidence in them.

The accounting models essentially just assume that all loans or investments by banks are funded by a combination of capital and debt/deposits. Moving to a higher capital ratio means switching a portion of the funding from cheaper debt to more expensive equity. The model simply calculates the increased funding costs on this simple accounting basis, which then may be fed into a model of the economy as a higher cost for borrowing by non-banks. These models may reduce the increased funding costs by an amount that partially reflects the Modigliani–Miller (M–M) theorem. In idealised circumstances, the theorem says the cost of any increase in the portion of more expensive capital will be precisely offset by reductions in the cost of each unit of capital and debt. In reality, this applies to a more limited extent. My own analysis suggests that about half of the offset does not occur due to violations of the theoretical assumptions in the real world.

The accounting model is fairly solid, but obviously leaves out any number of complicating factors and relies implicitly or explicitly on an estimate of the M–M theorem's effectiveness in real life.

At the other extreme, DGSE models are much more complicated mathematically and require a large number of assumptions about how finance and the wider economy work. They can be valuable tools, but it is always difficult to tell how well they reflect real life in the realm of financial regulation.

Given the reliance on theory rather than empirical study and the two big caveats, it is perhaps not surprising that there is a fairly wide range of estimates for the optimal capital levels from a societal point of view. The good news is that the Basel reforms put us somewhere in that range. I, personally, think the *aggregate* levels are broadly right, although I have many concerns about the details and implementation of the regulation.

Most of the overall cost-benefit analyses use the accounting model described earlier as the underlying basis for estimating the costs of higher capital requirements. The benefits of the higher requirements are usually estimated by looking at the relationship between aggregate capital levels and the probability of financial crisis. This is most often done by looking at the banking system as a whole as if it were essentially one bank, since we have extensive data on capital levels of banks and their subsequent failure rates. However, some analyses look at historical data for banking systems as a whole.

Calculating the benefits has its own further complexities, in that one must estimate the impact on the economy of financial crises, including the important question of how extensively and how quickly any reduction in the size of the economy is reversed. If there is a permanent reduction compared to what the growth track would have been, or if the output gap takes a long time to narrow, the economic costs of crisis will be much higher than if the damage is more short term.

I was the lead author in 2016 of a comprehensive literature review of studies of the costs of the Basel reforms (Elliott, et. al, 2016). Although the paper did not generally address the important question of the reforms' benefits, there is a brief review of existing cost-benefit analyses starting on page 83. The short version is that studies by academics and the official sector "resulted in estimated optimal levels [of capital] that range from 8% to over 20% of RWA" (that is, risk-weighted assets). Given the analytical complexities and the extent of required assumptions, it is not surprising that the range is so wide.

A further complication is that none of these studies considered the potential damage to financial stability if bank capital requirements are considerably higher than that for non-banks that can engage in many of the same activities. I, personally, worry considerably that if bank capital requirements were to be set at the high end of that 8% to 20% range, the system's safety would be considerably reduced by a flow of major portions of the business out of the banking sector into less regulated, and less well-capitalised, sectors.

Moving beyond the aggregate view, the details of regulation matter, not just the total capital and liquidity levels. This leaves us with further questions.

Third, what is well structured and what is less than optimal in the Basel reforms?

The overall thrust of the Basel reforms is clearly the right one; there should be considerably more capital than before the crisis and it should be of higher average quality, meaning more equity, and calculated on a basis that excludes equity supported by iffy assets. Few, if any, observers would argue with these two points.

Further, there is broad agreement that new liquidity requirements were needed to supplement capital standards. The crisis reminded us that liquidity can dry up rapidly in bad times and become very expensive when it is available.

Some of the pieces of the Basel reforms, however, have troublesome characteristics. I will confine myself to three of the larger issues, given space constraints. First, the strong move in the final stages of the Basel reforms to de-emphasise internal models carries the risk of overemphasising the relatively blunt risk bucket methodology used in the standard approach. Capital requirements that do not sufficiently differentiate among risks could push banks towards relatively riskier activities.

Second, the Net Stable Funding Ratio (NSFR) is substantially more arbitrary than the rest of the Basel standards. The capital rules in general are based on decades of experience, even if some aspects are quite new. The Liquidity Coverage Ratio (LCR), for its part, is intuitively clear in that it is a stylised stress test that uses a static balance sheet to make assumptions about cash flows in a crisis in order to ensure that a bank could survive 30 days until the cavalry rides over the hill to restore market liquidity through central bank and finance ministry interventions. In contrast, the NSFR is intended to push banks away from overly risky business models that rely on excessive maturity transformation. We do not, though, have a particularly good basis for deciding what is overly risky in this regard, so it is not clear that the chosen values for the NSFR calculations will achieve our purposes without forcing cutbacks in societally useful activities. This argues for ensuring that the calibration is less binding in order to eliminate only the extremes of behaviour, where we are sure dangers lie.

Third, the Basel reforms are heavily weighted towards the problems and needs of advanced economies. Emerging economies were invited to participate in a widened Basel Committee, but their net impact on the standards was fairly light. Part of this was the fault of the members from the advanced economies and part stems from an unwillingness of some emerging market nations to push harder and more effectively for their interests. Emerging market banks generally hold substantially higher capital levels than advanced economy banks as a result of market demands, their own caution and national regulations. These forces reflect the greater risk inherent in banking in emerging markets, with their various risks and crises. Since the Basel standards do not add an emerging market surcharge to capital requirements, they are rarely the binding capital constraints. Nonetheless, some distortions are created by having standards that are global, yet fundamentally designed with advanced economies in mind. See, for example, the oft-expressed concerns about how the Basel standards affect trade finance or the difficulty for some nations in finding enough High Quality Liquid Assets to satisfy the LCR and NSFR requirements.

Fourth, what is missing or only lightly touched upon in the Basel reforms?

The Basel Committee has acted on the large majority of areas of regulation directly involving capital and liquidity, with the prominent exception of the vexed question of establishing positive risk weights for sovereign bonds of advanced economies. (There the Basel Committee staff put forward their ideas, but without the backing of the Committee itself.)

Further, it has announced its intention to focus more on aligning supervisory standards around the world, on which it has done relatively little while it was wrestling with major regulatory changes.

Beyond capital, liquidity and supervision, there are a host of other areas important to the stability of banks and of the financial system as a whole. However, this falls outside of the Basel Committee's role, and would require a very extended treatise, so I will not touch on this further.

Fifth, what are the interactions between the Basel reforms and other regulation and supervision around the globe? Do we have too many measures trying to achieve the same ends?

There are a host of interactions between the Basel standards and national/regional regulation and supervision. This is inherent in the structure, given that: the Basel standards only cover capital and liquidity; they are intended to be minimum standards, leaving room for higher or supplementary requirements; and the Basel Committee is not a treaty organisation, so its recommendations are not legally binding on the member states. In practice, there are not only differences in national implementation of the Basel standards, including outright omissions in some cases of parts of the standards, but national implementation is embedded in a wider structure of regulation and supervision that differs country by country.

I'm confident we do have too many overlapping and sometimes conflicting measures, but the much tougher issues are about how to decide what should be dropped or modified and precisely how. Space does not allow a serious discussion of this here, but readers may refer to Elliott et al. (2016) for an extensive review of the interactions of the Basel standards and other financial regulations.

Conclusions

The important work of the Basel Committee unfortunately is not one that is easy to judge analytically and objectively. There are too many questions about how the financial system works and the impacts of capital and liquidity standards on the system, not to mention the many pages of details contained in the standards. Nonetheless, I am convinced that Basel III is a big step forward, despite a number of flaws that will hopefully be fixed over time.

Bibliography

Elliott, Douglas and Emre Balta, Vishal Abbhinand, Olivia Korostelina and Mehree Siddique, *Interaction, Coherence, and Overall Calibration of Post Crisis Basel Reforms*, August 2016, Oliver Wyman, available at www.oliverwyman.com

A summary by Douglas Elliott and Emre Balta was published in the Banque de France 2017 Financial Stability Review

V: What Basel III means to investors

Stuart Graham, Partner, Banks Strategy

The view of equity investors on Basel IV

I am very pleased to present the view of equity investors on what we call Basel IV (the finalisation of Basel III). As someone who has written almost 200 pages of research reports on Basel IV over the last few years, I have spent a lot of time talking with equity investors on the subject. My firm, Autonomous Research, has also conducted at least three detailed surveys of equity investors' views on Basel IV, which we have from time to time shared with the Basel Committee and other regulators.

Finality on Basel IV is very important

The first point I'd like to make is that finality on Basel IV is extremely important for equity investors. It is a water shed moment. In order to value a bank with confidence, equity investors need to know how much capital it requires. And for the last 10 years that figure has been subject to continual upward revision due to Basel 2.5, then Basel III and then Basel IV. For example, back in December 2009 (when the Basel III rules were first unveiled for consultation) we thought a core Tier 1 ratio of 8%–9% would be sufficient for an average European bank. We also thought that Basel III was the end point for post-crisis re-regulation. Now we typically assume a core Tier 1 ratio of 11%–13% on a risk-weighted asset base which will likely increase by a further + 10%–14% under Basel IV. On a broadly like-for-like basis, that would represent a potential increase in capital requirements by +60% since late 2009. The resultant uncertainty over capital requirements has raised the risk premium on bank equities, meaning a higher cost of equity. Most equity investors I talk to lost interest in the whole topic of a 70%, 72.5% or 75% output floor quite some time ago. The attitude for much of the last six months, for example, has been one of "why can't the regulators just fix a level – and let the banks get on with implementing it."

A period of regulatory calm is now called for

The second point I'd like to make is that equity investors expect regulators are now done and that there is no Basel V in prospect. Ten years is a long time in the careers of most equity investors. The crisis led to many job losses

https://doi.org/10.1515/9783110621495-012

amongst investors too. So there are many equity investors whose only knowledge of the Basel Committee is of a body which is constantly changing banks' capital requirements and adding to complexity and uncertainty in their equity investing decisions. We all know it was not always so. After Basel I was agreed, the Basel Committee basically went quiet for just over a decade. I think a similar period of quiet is now called for from the Basel Committee.

Many of you will be thinking – why the complaining by bank investors? The re-regulation was necessary. I 100% agree. But after 10 years of tweaking the rules, I strongly believe enough is enough. Regulators should now let the banks get on with implementation. To illustrate this point, let's take the example of Deutsche Bank, which went into the crisis 61 times levered in 2007. We have previously estimated that if Basel III had existed in 2007, Deutsche's stated Basel I CET1 ratio of 6.9% would have in fact been just 1.7% on a Basel III basis. On a Basel IV basis (had it existed back in 2007) we estimate Deutsche's CET1 ratio would have been even lower, at around 1.0%. Today, Deutsche's CET1 ratio is 13.8% and even on a fully loaded Basel IV basis we still think it will be 11.5%. However you look at it, Deutsche is way better capitalised now than it was pre-crisis. In my view, the Basel Committee can justifiably say "job done" on raising banks' capital levels.

We see the same picture if we look at the US banking industry – which was at the centre of the Great Financial Crisis. US banks' equity/asset ratios are back to the levels of the late 1930s (11.2%). We don't have core Tier 1 ratios going back very far for the US banking system (only back to 2001). But here too we can see that US banks' capital ratios are at unquestionably strong levels (12.6% versus a pre-crisis peak of 8.5%). It is notable that the Federal Reserve seems to have accepted this point, with many US banks now allowed to undertake 100% annual pay-outs of earnings (mainly through buy-backs, to be fair).

We think equity investors will front-load the very long phase-in periods

My third point is that equity investors will not care about the 2022–2027 phase-in period. The feedback we get from talking to equity investors and also from our formal surveys of investors is that they will front-load Basel IV. Most likely, we think that front-loading will take effect when the banks are first required to publish their new Standardised Risk-Weighted Assets ("RWAs") – most likely by the end of 2021, we think. When that figure is published, even the laziest bank analysts will be able to calculate the "as if fully loaded ratio" by taking 72.5% of the Standardised RWAs. In the meantime, calculating that figure from the outside is quite challenging, as shown by the relatively wide variance in analysts' estimates of banks' pro-forma Basel IV core Tier 1 ratios.

For example, in our last survey on Basel IV from early December 2017, the consensus answer on when equity investors would start applying Basel IV capital requirements was by the end of 2021. More investors signalled they would apply the requirements already in their own analysis in 2018 than did for the whole 2023–2027 period combined!

This front-loading view is justified, in our opinion, because although the Basel IV RWA inflation of likely +10%–14% for the European banks is painful, it is manageable. For example, even on a fully-loaded 2020 timetable, we don't see the need for any European bank to raise equity to meet Basel IV and we think only a handful of banks might need to dial back on current dividend or buy-back expectations. So the message to bank management teams from most equity investors we talk to is "get on with implementing Basel IV and get the regulator off your back."

This holds true even for the most impacted business models, in our view. The estimated average RWA inflation of +10%–14% hides a wide range of outcomes. We estimate impacts of +15%–30% on some European wholesale banks, and +30% for some mortgage banks and commercial real estate lenders in the north of Europe. However, many of these banks such as ABN AMRO in the Netherlands or Aareal in Germany have run with very high core Tier 1 ratios precisely because (a) they knew risk weightings could be revised upwards and (b) they need to comply with the Basel III Leverage Ratio. Interestingly these two banks have been most explicit in quantifying the impact of Basel IV, safe in the knowledge that they already maintain a sufficient capital buffer to deal with the forthcoming tougher requirements.

Equity investors now expect European bank pay-outs to increase

My fourth point is that equity investors expect banks to return increasing amounts of capital to them in the coming years. If we take the view that at some point between today and end 2021 (at the latest) all the European banks will have met their fully loaded Basel IV capital requirements, then they have no need to accumulate yet more capital.

We think the European banking sector in aggregate will make something like a 10%–12% RoTBV (return on tangible book value), given the likely course of interest rates (up a bit, but still very low by historic standards). The forward curve suggests 3-month Euribor will still only be at + 85 basis points by the end of 2021. RWA growth in this environment is likely to be in the + 2%–3% range (which compares to 8%+ in the mid-2000s). So in theory, banks should be able to pay out 70% of earnings in dividends and buy-backs and still be able to back likely RWA growth and keep the regulators happy. That is a big change from pre-crisis when European banks paid out 40%–50% of earnings in dividends. It is also a big change from the period 2009–2016 when bank dividend payouts were in the 20%–30% range. Put another way, for the last decade many banks have been run to please the regulators and bond-holders. Now many equity investors think post-Basel IV, it is their turn to share in the upside.

Some of you may feel it is unwise to let banks increase their dividend pay-outs. But I believe strongly it is also unwise to make them hoard capital they don't need. If regulators don't let banks develop an investment case aimed at value investors (via increasing dividends), they run the risk of perpetuating an unnecessarily high cost of equity for the sector.

There has been a lot of discussion at this conference about whether the banks hold enough capital. We can argue back and forth on the relative merits of 12%, 18% or 20% capital ratios. But those who argue for very high ratios should also consider how they expect the banks to achieve their cost of equity (usually thought to be around 10%) on such high capital bases. If banks cannot sustainably cover their cost of equity, then equity investors will not stand ready to subscribe for new equity capital. They will simply be throwing good money after bad. And how safe is the financial system if the banks all trade at discounts to book value and have no access to fresh equity and/or Additional Tier 1 capital?

Equity holders can be happy with banks making 10%–12% RoTBVs

My fifth and final point is that banks as utilities – 10% RoTBVs with 70% pay-outs – can be very attractive investments for equity investors. With a few exceptions (mainly those banks with exposure to emerging markets) it is almost impossible to make the case that banks are growth companies. There is too much debt in the world for that. So they must gear their investment appeal to value investors who are focused on dividend growth. Again, if you think about it, that is why you have heard so many investment professionals at various points over the last few years say "oh banks – they are simply uninvestable." Growth investors haven't liked them because there is no earnings growth story. Value investors haven't liked them either, because they have had no idea on where the capital rules would settle and therefore how dividends might grow.

But now, if equity investors can have much more clarity and confidence in banks' dividend growth potential, bank equities can rerate as the risk premium comes down. Well-run banks with clear dividend policies in Australia, Canada and Sweden trade on 12.5–13.5 times 2019 earnings. In my view, those economies are all very late in the cycle and the local banks have had it very good for a very long period of time. By contrast, European banks have gone through extremely tough times and now are facing an improving macro environment. After a long period of dividend uncertainty, they at long last look like they could be facing some certainty. And yet they trade on 11.5 times 2019 earnings. So the bull case for European banks is that the equities can rerate higher as capital uncertainty gives way to clarity.

There are many complications along the way

The above narrative sounds deceptively simple. We all know that formal Basel implementation can be fiendishly complex in Europe. In particular, it is well known that the Basel Committee has deemed the European Union to be "materially non-compliant" on Basel III. Given how hard many EU policy makers lobbied against Basel IV, it is only logical to conclude that it too will be materially watered down when translated into EU law. So the EU could be "materially non-compliant squared." This process of translating Basel IV into EU law is unlikely to start until 2020 at the earliest, by which stage memories of 2007–09 will have dimmed yet further.

In this context, we note that several large European banks declined to give a Basel IV RWA inflation estimate with their fourth quarter 2017 results, noting that the rules would likely change when implemented in the EU. While such statements are understandable (and very probably true), they merely serve to perpetuate the uncertainty, in our view. We would have preferred the banks to give the Basel impacts, thereby allowing investors to consider likely worst case outcomes – which we believe to be manageable in any case.

More capital isn't everything

Although we have focused on capital in our comments, we are big believers in the view that more capital isn't the be all and end all. Resolvability and liquidity are also highly important for banking regulation.

In this context we can observe that Basel III has unquestionably made the banks safer. For example, back in 2007, the average global systemically important bank had a liquidity reserve of just $60bn. Today that figure is well over $200bn.

With regard to resolvability, we think that so-called living wills and total loss absorbing capital are very helpful tools. But we have seen in Europe, in cases such as Banco Popular and Vicenza/Veneto, that resolving even quite small banks is still an extremely complicated process.

Summary

In conclusion, most equity investors I talk with feel that Basel IV is the watershed moment they have been waiting for to begin that gradual rerating process of bank equities. I see no prospects for a Basel V and nor do I think such a further bout of re-regulation is necessary.

Laurie Mayers, Associate Managing Director, Moody's Investors Service

Credit implications of Basel III – the analyst and investor's perspective

Greater comparability of Pillar I risk-weighted assets

The agreement on Basel III will aid analysts and investors in their comparative analysis of banks removing key drivers of divergence in Pillar I risk weights. The differences in banks' RWA models have led to differences in Pillar I capital held for similar risks, undermining investors' confidence in the Basel III framework. In reaction to this, as well as in order to address deemed deficiencies in Pillar I for risks not captured or not fully captured, regulators have taken varying approaches to assessing additional capital. Sometimes these assessments of incremental capital were added to Pillar I RWAs, which are disclosed, but in other cases, these assessments were achieved through the use of Pillar II, which is often not disclosed or if disclosed, not broken down by risk type. These issues have made bank analysis more difficult and created the necessity for bank analysts and investors alike to become experts in the different ways regulators across jurisdictions have implemented Basel II and III. Because of the introduction of standardised output floors, the removal of the ability to use internal models for determining RWAs for low default portfolios as well as the enhancement of the standardised approach for operational risk, the agreement on Basel III will enhance comparability of banks' Pillar I RWA disclosures. We expect that these enhancements will also reduce, although not eliminate regulators' use of Pillar II capital assessments to "top up Pillar I," further enhancing comparability of Pillar I RWAs.

Extent of harmonization of jurisdictional implementation will determine the extent to which greater comparability is achieved

As with Basel II and the previous aspects of Basel III, the extent of comparability that will be achieved as a result of the Basel Committee's most recent agreement will be a function of how these changes are translated into rules at the jurisdic-

https://doi.org/10.1515/9783110621495-013

tional level. Comparative analysis of banks is not just done within jurisdictions but for many peers across jurisdictions as well. Therefore, bank analysts and investors will have a keen interest in seeing the extent to which the implementation of Basel III is harmonised particularly at the European level and in the United States both in terms of scope and transition periods. To the extent that the approach to implementation varies across jurisdictions, analysts and investors will have to understand these differences. At the time of this writing, the outcome in this regard is still not clear.

Transition periods will give banks time to adjust

Prior to the agreement being reached on Basel III, many banks, particularly the more complex global banks, were already estimating material increases in their regulatory capital requirements with this RWA inflation being reflected in their capital plans. Banks already challenged by the introduction of leverage constraints and material increases in capital requirements as a result of previous post-crisis reforms were now faced with further capital increases and the need to further optimize capital usage. Capital plans reflected these challenges with further enhancements of data and models as well as trade compression and netting being planned to offset the estimated RWA increases. The recent agreement not only provides greater clarity to banks as to the scope of the changes but also due to the transition periods proposed will give banks more time to adjust. Banks will be able to spend the next few years further enhancing their capital and operational efficiency, thereby increasing organic capital generation prior to the beginning of the implementation period for these most recent changes to Basel III. While enhancements to banks' solvency metrics provide greater protection for bond holders, a credit positive, additional challenges to banks' business models put further pressure on businesses already under strain. So the longer transition periods will give banks more time to execute their strategies and to adjust positioning them more favorably for the further regulatory pressures to come. While capital plans may now no longer reflect an immediate increase in RWAs from these most recent changes just agreed, banks are not being complacent and know that they must be prepared, in due course, for both these pressures and those that will likely result from the fundamental review of the trading book, on which further work is planned by the Basel Committee.

Comparability in Europe will be further enhanced by initiatives of the ECB

In the EU, in addition to the enhanced comparability and transparency that will be achieved on the back of the most recent Basel III reforms, initiatives of the ECB will also support these objectives. In particular, the ECB's initiative under its targeted review of internal models (TRIM) to ensure that internal models that are appropriately designed, calibrated and validated will likely lead to capital increases for many banks. Consistency in the robustness of internal models, in cases where their use will still be permitted, will further enhance analysts' and investors' confidence in bank disclosures and the comparability of bank capital levels.

Does Basel III mean the end of internal models

The introduction of output floors and the inability to use internal models when determining regulatory capital requirements for low default portfolios, credit valuation adjustments (CVA) and operational risk beg the question as to whether banks will continue to use these models for risk management and pricing of risk. Our view is that most banks will have already experienced the benefits of risk adjusted pricing and risk adjusted monitoring of risk. In fact, many smaller banks that do not have regulatory approval for use of internal models for credit risk run these models in parallel for risk management purposes. In addition, some larger banks that do not presently use the Advanced Measurement Approach for operational risk capital calculations run these models internally due to the fact that these frameworks enhance their monitoring and management of operational risk. What the Basel III changes do mean, however, is that bank analysts and investors will need to continue to understand not only how banks calculate capital for different risk types but also the tools and frameworks they use to manage and price risk, particularly as the capital framework becomes less risk sensitive.

Less risk sensitivity increases the importance of comprehensive supervision

As the regulatory capital framework becomes less risk sensitive, particularly with the introduction of output floors and the inability to use internal models for certain types of risks and exposures, comprehensive and in-depth supervision of banks takes on increased importance. While adequate solvency levels provide protection for bond holders, minimising the probability of a bank's default, effective governance, risk assessment and management of current and emerging risks is essential for the sustainability of banks. Supervisors therefore will play an increasingly important role in ensuring not only that banks remain adequately capitalised but that they have effective three lines of defence risk frameworks, robust firm-wide stress testing and capital planning processes as well as appropriate governance of funding and liquidity risk. Supervisory focus on adequate provisioning for non-performing loans (NPLs) and effective strategies for the reduction of NPLs, which are a drag on bank profitability, are also important areas to support banks' solvency.

Summary

The agreement recently achieved on Basel III is credit positive for analysts and investors from Moody's point of view as the revised capital framework will enhance the comparability and transparency of banks' capital disclosures. While the changes will fall unevenly on European banks, depending on the complexity and mix of their business models, the clarity the agreement provides will remove a major element of uncertainty for banks and those who follow them. The relatively long transition periods will give banks more time to adjust. Of course, the final impact of the agreement reached at the level of the Basel Committee will not fully be known until there is greater clarity on the extent to which what has been agreed will be implemented at the jurisdictional level, particularly in Europe and the United States.

Levin Holle, German Federal Ministry of Finance, Head of Financial Markets Policy Department

What Basel III means to investors?

A distinguished panel looking at Basel III from the investor's perspective included *Laurie Mayers* of Moody's Europe, Associate Managing Director in Moody's European Banking team, *Stuart Graham*, founding partner of Autonomous Research, a specialist global research firm for financial services companies, and *Philippe Bodereau* of PIMCO Europe, managing director and portfolio manager, global head of PIMCO's financial research. Panellists analysed expected effects on and reactions of investors from a broader analysts' perspective, but also more specifically focusing on equity and bond investors in financial institutions.

There was a general sense of welcome of the Basel accord in terms of ending regulatory uncertainty, but the discussion also reminded of the importance of a full and even implementation across jurisdictions in order to achieve the objectives of reducing risk variability and enhancing comparability, also for investors. Whereas the finalisation of Basel III was conceived as a substantial contribution to comparability and transparency particular for banks' internal models, the need for continued supervisory review as well as independent stress-testing and analysis was clearly pointed out.

The debate evidenced a trade-off between the interests of equity investors and bond holders, the former expecting banks to quickly overcome the Basel challenge and then return payouts or buy-backs, the latter requiring a stable and comforting equity base securely preventing a bail-in of bond holders. The changes in risk-weighted assets show a wide range of outcomes for different business models inducing investors to follow closely the reaction of the banks most concerned. Bond investors will pay particular attention to how banks will live up to the challenges of Basel III and in parallel manage the building up of TLAC and market the corresponding eligible debt instruments.

In conclusion there was agreement that the investors' view adds a valuable dimension to assess the new Basel accord. Investors' assessment confirmed that it was high time to finalise Basel III, that a truthful and even implementation throughout jurisdictions is now needed and that both equity and bond investors expect European banks to responsibly manage the required adjustments. Investors recognise a margin of manoeuvre and a sufficient time frame for implementation and adaptation. However, they perceived it as limited and expressed their preference addressing the new challenges in a consistent and timely manner. Looking forward beyond Basel III implementation, it was generally acknowledged

https://doi.org/10.1515/9783110621495-014

that different challenges, mainly digitalisation and the importance of the growing Asian financial sector, might have an even more important impact on the shape and development of the European banking sector.

VI: The geographic consequences

Sandie O'Connor, Chief Regulatory Affairs Officer, JPMorgan Chase & Co.

Basel agreed, so what's next?

The international banking system has undergone a lengthy period of post-crisis regulatory change with an overhaul of the prudential framework at its core. There is no doubt that post-crisis reforms, particularly those increasing the quantity and quality of capital, have been key to strengthening the banking system. The recent finalisation of Basel III revisions provides certainty on the minimum standards for the global framework and serves as the foundation for financial stability across jurisdictions and markets. The ability to reach an agreement is a strong reaffirmation by member countries of their commitment to achieving consistent and comparable standards for internationally active financial institutions. It was important to achieve certainty on what the complete framework looks like.

However, there is still more to do – we must remember that Basel III is not legally binding and jurisdictions must now finalise their own rule-makings, so the important work lies ahead for local policymakers and regulators to consistently and coherently implement these standards. Each jurisdiction will face unique challenges in implementation, whether it's complexity due to the interaction with existing statute or impacts due to different starting points. Nonetheless, consistent implementation will be vital for savers, investors, markets and economic growth.

The primary goals of the Basel III reforms were to restore credibility in the calculation of risk-weighted assets (RWA) by reducing variability in their calculation, improving the comparability of banks' capital ratios by ensuring that banks capitalise the same risks the same way, and accomplishing this in as simple a way as possible. While the minimum standards apply evenly to all, we need to recognise that starting points vary and therefore the impact on individual banks and jurisdictions will be different. Core factors that drive differences in impact include an institution's size; business model, including composition of its book across credit, market and operating businesses; and its existing capital requirements and position. For example, firms with larger trading books may be more impacted than those with less capital markets activity. Despite expected differences in short-term impact, progress against the Basel III goals is only achievable if the minimum standards are implemented consistently in each jurisdiction.

https://doi.org/10.1515/9783110621495-015

The U.S. take – A shorter road to compliance, but what implementation obstacles await?

When examining the impact of the recently finalised reforms on U.S. banks, existing capital requirements are arguably the most relevant factor to consider. The preemptive implementation of "U.S. Basel III" in 2013[1] was largely a reaction to the financial crisis and incorporated statutory capital-related provisions in the Dodd-Frank Act. It included a number of requirements that were, and still are, substantially more stringent than international standards in a number of areas, such as the introduction of an enhanced supplementary leverage ratio that includes a buffer on top of the leverage ratio for the largest banks. Additionally, investors expected firms to promptly adapt to these heightened capital requirements. As a result, U.S. banks now find themselves already compliant with a prudential framework that in most respects already meets or exceeds the newly finalised global standards. U.S. banks' "distance to compliance" with these new minimum standards is generally less than that of international peers; however, they face their own unique set of challenges relating to U.S. implementation.

One of the more complex issues to navigate when U.S. regulators begin implementing these new standards is the fact that certain U.S. requirements are codified in the Dodd-Frank Act legislation and cannot be adjusted by regulatory agencies. For example, a provision known as the "Collins" floor[2] introduced a statutory capital floor which is different – both in calibration and in construct – from the output floor just finalised by Basel.[3] Secondly, the Dodd-Frank Act eliminated credit ratings in financial regulations,[4] effectively prohibiting reliance

1 Federal Reserve Board (2013): Regulatory Capital Rules: Regulatory Capital, Implementation of Basel III, Capital Adequacy, Transition Provisions, Prompt Corrective Action, Standardized Approach for Risk-weighted Assets, Market Discipline and Disclosure Requirements, Advanced Approaches Risk-Based Capital Rule, and Market Risk Capital Rule; Final Rule, https://www.federalreserve.gov/newsevents/pressreleases/bcreg20130702a.htm. The rule implemented Basel II and Basel III in the United States.

2 Dodd-Frank Wall Street Reform and Consumer Protection Act (Dodd-Frank Act), Pub. L. No. 111–203, §171, 124 Stat. 1436 (21 July 2010)

3 The Collins floor is calibrated at 100%, but the Basel floor is calibrated at a maximum of 72.5% after the phase-in period. The composition of the floors also differ; the Collins floor compares the sum of RWAs calculated using the standardized approach for credit and market risk with the sum of RWAs calculated using the advanced approach for credit, market and operational risk; the Basel floor compares the sum of RWAs calculated using the standardized approach with the sum of RWAs calculated using the advanced approach across all risk stripes.

4 Dodd-Frank Wall Street Reform and Consumer Protection Act (Dodd-Frank Act), Pub. L. No. 111–203, §939A, 124 Stat. 1885 (July 21 2010)

on them for RWA calculations. This results in U.S. banks having to fall back to higher required levels of capital, even on investment grade positions, for both standardised and advanced capital requirements. Although it is helpful that the final Basel standards provide a "non-ratings based" approach for jurisdictions that cannot rely on credit ratings, this approach is comparatively less granular than the ratings-based approach, resulting in divergent risk weightings for the same risk across jurisdictions. Jurisdictional constraints will add complexity to implementation and undoubtedly make complete comparability between banks' RWAs difficult to achieve. However, global regulators must continue to strive for as much cross-jurisdictional consistency as possible to manage against a greater fragmentation of markets, competitive disadvantages or regulatory arbitrage.

So does Basel III matter for U.S. banks?

Yes, a consistent minimum standard has value for all market participants and financial stability. Most jurisdictions are still at a very early stage of local implementation so precise implications are not yet clear. If Basel III is implemented in the United States as finalised, aggregate capital levels may not increase since large U.S. banks will generally be bound by constraints other than the new Basel III standards. However, due to the granularity of its components, Basel III specific requirements could be higher for some products and services, which may affect the way banks allocate capital and the provision of those products and services. This becomes particularly important if Basel III is binding; as we know, the binding constraint of today may not be the binding constraint of tomorrow.

We're not done yet...

The Basel III standard is "final" – but the work is not complete and should not stop here. As already noted, local implementation is being defined and banks will continue to evolve their business models and activities in response to the new rules, their own risk appetite and shareholder return objectives. Therefore, it will be important for local regulators and Basel to continue performing robust quantitative impact studies to understand how banks, the economy and the markets are reacting to both new and existing regulations. In particular, analyses are needed to identify emerging concentration risk or changes in banking activity, such as the movement away from certain segments or types of products offered, especially if those changes are unintended. The framework provides adequate durability and flexibility over time, but Basel must continue regular and ongoing monitoring to make adjustments as appropriate.

Encouragingly, global regulators have been in an ongoing state of assessment with regards to FRTB since its finalization several years ago, and have appropriately opted to extend the implementation timeline for the revised market risk framework in an effort to address detailed calibration issues at an international level.[5] We are supportive of Basel tackling these issues at a global level, as it will help limit the potential for significantly divergent approaches to implementation at a local level.

Perhaps most importantly, with Basel III finalised, now is the appropriate time for a comprehensive review of the broader regulatory framework to determine its overall coherence. Until now, rules have been calibrated in isolation and studies on coherence have been limited to subsets of the framework or jurisdiction-specific impacts. We encourage policymakers to continue assessing what has been put into place with the goal of making existing financial regulation more effective and efficient without sacrificing the safety and soundness of the system.

Finally, there are also improvements that can be made to the rule-making process to ensure deeper engagement and collaboration between regulators and banks at both the local and international levels. We've completed the big pieces of post-crisis reforms, but that shouldn't prevent us from thinking about how we can increase transparency, accountability, and empirical analysis so that the views and concerns of all stakeholders are appropriately considered and taken into account as we continue to work to strengthen the global financial system.

5 On March 22, Basel issued for consultation revisions to the minimum capital requirements for market risk. https://www.bis.org/press/p180322.htm

Christian Ossig, Chief Executive of the Association of German Banks

Geographic consequences of Basel III: effects on Europe

1 Introduction

The finalisation in December 2017 of Basel III (or "Basel IV") is a major milestone in the response by the Basel Committee on Banking Supervision (BCBS) to the financial crisis (Section 2). Standards which are as uniform as possible throughout the world are a major and precious asset. Consistent implementation of the framework in Europe is therefore crucially important to all European banks. Nevertheless, when the new Basel framework is implemented in Europe, European specificities and the anticipated substantial quantitative impact on the level of capital requirements in Europe (Section 3) demand a certain number of adaptations. This article explains why European banks will be particularly affected and describes the nature of the European specificities. They lie primarily in the specific business and risk profile of European banks (Section 4), their good experience with the internal ratings-based (IRB) approach (Section 5) and the solution Europe has already found to the problem of variability in internal model results (Section 6). From this basis, we derive recommendations for European implementation in the new Capital Requirements Regulation, CRR III (Section 7).

2 Basel resolution of December 2017: finalising post-crisis reforms

The document "Basel III: Finalising post-crisis reforms," published on 7 December 2017, is rightly regarded by stakeholders as a major milestone in the Basel Committee's response to the financial crisis. It is not the Committee's last word, however. Work on finalising the Fundamental Review of the Trading Book (FRTB),

---

Note: Disclaimer: the positions expressed in this article are those of the author and do not necessarily reflect the position of the Association of German Banks (Bundesverband deutscher Banken). I would like to thank my colleagues Uwe Gaumert and Michaela Zattler for their valuable contribution to this paper.

https://doi.org/10.1515/9783110621495-016

for instance, will not be completed before the end of 2018 at the earliest (a new consultation document was published in March 2018). This is most certainly part of the Basel III framework, in our view. The Pillar 1 treatment of sovereign exposures is also an issue likely to remain unresolved for the foreseeable future.

The first part of Basel III (final document issued in December 2010 and revised in June 2011) substantially strengthened the capital adequacy of banks and introduced liquidity standards. Its primary focus was not on how risk-weighted assets (RWAs) are calculated. By contrast, the second part concentrates above all on adjustments at RWA level. Given the scale of the modifications involved – as well as the huge impact these are expected to have on the banks – there is definitely a case for calling the project "Basel IV." The most recent revision of the Basel framework was driven largely by criticism of banks' internal models and the variability in their results under Pillar 1. It is both legitimate and sensible to try to reduce the variability and we support this objective. Views nevertheless differ on how it can best be achieved.

In the areas of credit valuation adjustment (CVA) and operational risk, the use of model approaches will no longer be permitted while the use of the IRB approach will be restricted for certain asset classes. The new framework goes as far as removing the advanced (A-IRB) approach for low-default portfolios and even dropping the IRB approach altogether (for equity exposures).

Stefan Ingwes, Chairman of the Basel Committee, put the objective of December's document as follows: "These reforms will help reduce excessive variability in risk-weighted assets and will improve the comparability and transparency of banks' risk-based capital ratios" (press release on the publication, page 1). The document comprises the following elements:

- a revised standardised approach to credit risk with slightly improved risk sensitivity,
- a revised IRB approach, which restricts the scope of the approach and introduces input floors,
- a revised CVA framework, including the removal of the model approach and the introduction of a new standardised approach,
- a revised framework for operational risk, replacing the advanced measurement approaches (AMA) and introducing a new standardised approach,
- revisions to the leverage ratio framework and
- an aggregate RWA-based output floor covering all risk categories and sets at 72.5%.

This article focuses solely on the standardised approach to credit risk, the IRB approach, the output floor and on how these three elements interact with one another. A look at the exact definition of the output floor will be helpful for this purpose. Here is the formula:

$$\sum RW\,As\,(basis{:}\ internal\ models) + \sum RW\,As\,(basis{:}\ standardised\ approaches) \geq 0.725\left(\sum RW\,As\,(basis{:}\ standardised\ approaches)\right)$$

On the left-hand side of the equation are, as expected, the RWAs calculated by internal models using the prescribed calculation formulae (first sum). The second sum on the left-hand side of the equation represents all the RWAs for which the bank has no model approval (partial use or no model approach available) or, in other words, RWAs calculated using standardised approaches. On the right-hand side of the equation is the sum of RWAs calculated under all standardised approaches using the prescribed calculation formulae.

3 Anticipated consequences for capital requirements in the EU

The consequences of the Basel reforms were hotly debated in 2016 and 2017. Various impact studies by the Basel Committee, accounting firms, management consultancies and banking associations reached different conclusions about the expected increase in RWAs worldwide. But all these studies found that RWAs were likely to rise more for European banks than for banks in other major financial centres around the world. The anticipated rises in Europe were not, moreover, consistent with the objective formulated by policymakers that the reforms should not lead to substantial increases. An “insignificant” increase in RWAs of at most 10% was posited.

The most robust estimates for Europe were issued on a best-efforts basis by the European Banking Authority (EBA) in December 2017 (EBA 2017). The impact assessment used out-of-date portfolio data from December 2015. It was carried out on a sample of 88 European banks from 17 countries, 36 of these banks had total assets exceeding 30 billion euros (Group 1 banks). The EBA chose a sound approach for the assessment by comparing the Basel framework as currently implemented in the CRR/CRD IV with the requirements set out in the final Basel document of 7 December 2017 as far as this was possible on the basis of the available data. For a number of reasons, however, the resulting figures need to be treated with caution. For one thing, the Basel document contains a number of new and sometimes not totally clear-cut definitions, whose precise interpretation is likely to have a significant effect on the overall results. And for another thing, these figures do not show the impact of the FRTB. Nor is it clear whether the reform of the standardised approach for measuring counterparty credit risk (SA-CCR, BCBS 279 issued in 2014) was taken into account. Yet both reforms will have significant effects on the end result. The FRTB and SA-CCR are currently in the process of being implemented in European law. It is already clear that the FRTB will result in a considerable increase in RWAs for market risk, especially at banks using internal models to calculate capital requirements. Calculating exposure amounts using the SA-CCR will normally lead to higher RWAs in affected portfolios as well. It is consequently safe to assume that the figures in the EBA's assessment would be exceeded in an analysis covering all aspects of the new framework. It should, however, be borne in mind that the pressure on business models exerted by the new rules will probably prompt banks to make adjustments (by restructuring portfolios, for example) and that these countermeasures may make the quantitative impact seem less severe. In a dynamic environment, the ceteris paribus assumption does not hold true.

The EBA found that the banks taking part in the survey would see their Tier 1 capital requirement rise by an average of 12.9%. At some banks, however, the increase might be much higher. The survey showed that Europe's significant (Group 1) banks would need an average of 14.1% more Tier 1 capital. For banks with total assets of less than 30 billion euros (Group 2 banks), on the other hand, the Tier 1 capital requirement would rise by only 3.9% on average. Owing to the small number of Group 2 banks in the sample compared to the total number of these institutions operating in Europe, it cannot be assumed that these figures are really representative. Above all, the question arises as to the reasons for the comparatively modest increase.

For the Group 1 banks, the output floor was the most important determining factor. It was responsible for an average rise of 6.9% in the CET 1 requirement, which represents around half of the total increase. In addition, the revised IRB approach for credit risk caused requirements to rise by 4.5% on average while a 2.7% average increase stemmed from operational risk reforms. It is highly probable that the latter increase was caused by the removal of the advanced measurement approaches. Since most of the Group 2 banks do not use internal models, the output floor led to an average increase of only 4.2% and the introduction of the new standardised approach for operational risk to an average increase of 0.8%. The most striking aspect, however, was a drop of 2.4% on average in the capital requirement for credit risk calculated under the standardised approach. In the absence of more detailed information, one can only speculate about the reasons for this decrease. We assume, however, that the need for less Tier 1 capital determined under the standardised approach to credit risk can mainly be explained by the choice of valuation method used for residential and commercial property loans.

It can be concluded, in summary, that big banks, which in Europe mainly use internal models, will be much harder hit by the reforms than will smaller banks. On top of that, it will clearly not be possible to achieve the objective, reaffirmed in summer 2016 by the European Council of Ministers, of an insignificant rise in capital requirements in Europe. The possible consequences of the reforms therefore need to be actively addressed. For this reason, we warmly welcome the European Commission's plan to conduct a thorough quantitative impact study (QIS) in 2018 since the increase in RWAs in Europe under "as is" implementation of the Basel framework can only be properly analysed on the basis of more precise and up-to-date figures. Should the QIS results indicate a significant increase in RWAs, adaptations of the Basel requirements will be essential if the Council of Ministers' objective is to be realised.

The European QIS should compare all aspects of the reforms which have not yet been implemented in EU law with the current situation under the CRR/CRD IV. This means including the FRTB, the SA-CCR, the standardised approach for operational risk, the standardised and IRB approaches for credit risk, the new CVA framework and the output floor. When it comes to the FRTB, account could also be taken of the findings of the Basel working group currently revisiting this issue. In addition, all the national discretions included in the framework should be analysed separately. And the highest possible level of granularity should be used for defining asset classes and sub-classes and for the various available approaches (e.g., loan to value versus loan-splitting approach).

4 Specificities of European banks – business and risk profile

Compared to other major financial centres, the European financial market is characterised by some important basic features which need to be taken into account when designing an appropriate regulatory regime for banks. The following observations relate primarily to banking book transactions.

The vast majority of investments in Europe are funded through the intermediation of banks. Bank loans account for 82% of all debt financing in the euro area and are generally preferred over capital market-based sources of finance (Ossig 2017). Since banks are the primary source of finance in Europe, they provide funding for investments of all maturities and normally hold these in their books until they mature. This is because the European secondary loan markets, like the primary capital markets, are comparatively underdeveloped. On top of that, the European securitisation market was badly hit in the wake of the financial crisis which started in 2007. Europe does not have government-backed agencies like Freddie Mac and Fannie Mae in the United States, to which banks can transfer risk in order to reduce their need for capital. As a result, a feature of European bank balance sheets is the high proportion of long-term assets. In 2017, 55% of all loans in the eurozone had a term of over 5 years (ECB 2018). The RWAs associated with such long-term positions therefore have a strong influence on banks' need for capital and cannot be adjusted at short notice.

A further factor determining the balance sheets of European banks is the funding of small- and medium-sized enterprises (SMEs). Over 99% of all companies in the EU are SMEs and two-thirds of all employees in the private sector work for SMEs (Ossig 2015). Most of these companies cannot afford an external rating or are unwilling to pay the associated costs. In consequence, they are dependent on banks to obtain funding. Conversely, a large proportion of banks' RWAs is made up of loans to unrated SMEs.

Property finance is another important business segment for European banks. Of all loans granted in 2017, 35% were used to buy or build residential property. Residential real estate finance accounts for 62% – and thus the lion's share – of long-term loans (5 years or more) in the eurozone (ECB 2018). On top of that, a substantial proportion of the commercial property sector is financed through banks. Owing to the special features of this business segment, it is often handled by specialised institutions.

The risks carried on the balance sheets of European banks therefore emanate to a large extent from property finance. Property markets differ, however, not only in comparison with the US but also across Europe, and sometimes widely so. Differences are especially apparent with respect to the following four factors, which all have a significant influence on the risk involved:

1. Definition of ownership rights
2. Enforceability of legal claims
3. Loan approval criteria and lending practices
4. Property valuation methods

In a few European countries, land register entries are not always available, either because they do not exist or because the authorities do not maintain them properly. In other countries, laws designed to protect tenants and homeowners prevent or prolong foreclosures, or the legal system is so inefficient that it takes many years to liquidate collateral. National standards for approving loans can also differ widely. There are basically two approaches: either to focus on the ability to sell the collateral as a means of reducing the exposure to loss, or to look at the borrower's ability to repay the loan from their income or other assets. Both approaches are used to a greater or lesser extent depending on the country involved. Finally, there are different procedures, with differing degrees of conservatism, for determining the value of a property. Standards on the frequency of property revaluations also differ.

Germany, for example, has a conservative approach to valuing property, namely the loan to value method. When assessing a loan application, the borrower's ability to repay the loan plays a key role. The liquidation of the collateral for a loan can be effectively enforced. For these reasons, losses on property loans have always been very low.

Up to now, risk-sensitive methods of determining the need for regulatory capital have been able to reflect these European specificities very well. Internal models have enabled individual probabilities of default to be estimated for borrowers without external ratings. The special features of national property markets have been reflected in different loss rates. In consequence, the widespread use of internal models by European banks may be regarded as a sound response to the market environment and explains the basically positive attitude of European supervisors to the IRB approach.

5 European experience with the IRB approach

Since the implementation in Europe of Basel II, European experience of the IRB approach has been extensive and positive. Unlike with market risk models, there has been no fundamental criticism of the performance of the IRB models. Nor has there been any systematic understatement of risk. A few critics have merely accused models of failing to adjust their estimates swiftly enough either in economic downturns or in upswings. There are legitimate reasons for these delays, however, the most important being requirements set by supervisors and the need for internal risk management to assess risk on a medium- to long-term basis so as to enable a comparatively long-term calculation of losses. Accusations of procyclicality are similarly unfounded and are explicitly no longer levelled by the EBA. Moreover, it should be mentioned that a countercyclical capital buffer of up to 2.5% was introduced in 2016 as a macro-prudential supervisory tool to counteract the risk of excessive credit growth. It should not be forgotten, finally, that the introduction of IRB models by banks when implementing Basel II has brought significant improvements to the quality of quantitative risk measurement and risk management. The disciplining effect of supervisory requirements and the resulting improvements in data collection and data quality have also helped banks make significant progress in risk management. What is more, European banks have invested, and continue to invest, enormous sums in obtaining and retaining permission to use their models. Models need to be continuously reviewed and refined – not least in the banks' own interests.

Originally, the key objectives, set by supervisors and pursued by banks a matter of course, were that models should focus on the individual portfolio (made-to-measure, not off-the-rack approach) and be as risk sensitive as possible. The recently expressed objective of making banks' risk estimations comparable was previously accorded little importance.

In addition, different countries have interpreted certain aspects of the CRR in very different ways. Take, for example, the definition of default, the estimation of the probability of default (PD) and the estimation of the level of loss in the event of default (loss given default, LGD). Some of these differences continue to persist.

True, all EU member states apply the same definition of default set out in Article 178 of the CRR. But although this provides a certain amount of standardisation and consistency, there are still various national discretions and differences in interpretation and interpretation guidance. This applies, for example, to calculating "days past due" (materiality, counting rules),
- the treatment of immaterial exposures,
- recovery with loss (has a default occurred or not?),
- capital requirements for defaulted exposures,
- rules on cure periods and
- assigning PDs following recovery.

When it comes to PD estimations, supervisors have set different requirements in areas such as
- cyclical adjustments in both directions, for example, in the event of a short historical observation period,
- margins of conservatism (MOCs) for model risk, for example, in low-default portfolios and
- length and weighting of data histories.

There are similar differences between supervisors' requirements for LGD estimation. These concern, for example,
- the level of application of the LGD floor,
- margins for model risk if data is scarce,
- monitoring satisfaction of the downturn requirement and
- the length and weighting of data histories.

In addition, banks make legitimate individual decisions about processes and during the development of their models. Even though the Basel Committee itself has found the ranking of debtors to be extremely consistent across banks, levels of PD and LGD estimation differ. These levels reflect different historical default experience and consequently cannot be objected to. Differences also arise as a result of a bank's decision to apply a point-in-time (PIT), through-the-cycle (TTC) or mixed rating approach. Such differences should not be eliminated.

Different PD and LGD estimates can also stem from different operational procedures. Initiating a debt recovery process at a very early stage can help prevent technical and minor defaults, for example. This influences both PD and LGD estimations. Responding to early warning indicators often makes it possible to reduce unsecured exposures before default occurs. Here, too, banks differ in how quickly they take action. Finally, success in liquidating collateral (in terms of the time needed, amount realised) depends on the quality of the liquidation procedures. These differences have an effect on LGD estimation.

The consequence of all this is a variability in results, which is now being criticised by regulators and supervisors although they themselves are largely responsible for it. The differences can be satisfactorily explained by economic, regulatory-driven and technical factors and cannot be put down to inappropriate modelling. Even where identical test portfolios are involved, some amount of variability is hardly surprising and by no means shocking.

The ECB was entrusted with the task of supervising eurozone banks in 2014. The standardisation of the rules on using internal models (Targeted Review of Internal Models – TRIM) and the activities of the EBA (standard-setting, benchmarking) will reduce variability and improve comparability. This is explored in more depth in the next section.

6 European answer to the variability problem

In Europe, a cause-based approach focusing on model estimates themselves has been pursued for some time now to adequately address the variability problem. This is the right approach and an appropriate European response without eroding the meaningfulness of models by way of floors.

The approach aimed at reducing undue variability in model results essentially comprises three elements that are presented in the following:

- EBA work on IRB approach-related standardisation through regulatory technical standards (RTSs) and guidelines (GLs), for example, on the definition of default, on PD and LGD parameter estimation with uniform treatment of model uncertainties by way of margin of conservatism requirements, on supervisory approval to use the IRB approach,
- benchmarking in accordance with Article 78 of CRD IV and
- the TRIM exercise 2017–2019.

EBA work on IRB approach-related standardisation: mention must be made in this respect particularly of various RTSs and GLs:

- Guidelines on the application of the definition of default (harmonisation of the definition of default using the "90 days past due" criterion and the "unlikeliness to pay" criterion)
- Regulatory technical standards on the assessment methodology for the IRB approach (harmonisation of supervisory approval of IRB models)
- Guidelines on PD estimation, LGD estimation and the treatment of defaulted exposures (most comprehensive EBA guideline containing detailed requirements for PD estimation [e.g., MOCs for various model estimation uncertainties in PD estimation], on LGD estimation and on the treatment of defaulted exposures)
- Regulatory technical standards on the specification of the nature, severity and duration of an economic downturn in accordance with Articles 181(3)(a) and 182(4)(a) of Regulation (EU) No 575/2013 (harmonisation of the definition of "downturn" for LGD estimation)
- Regulatory technical standards on the materiality threshold of credit obligations past due (harmonisation of the definition and the design of the materiality threshold using the "90 days past due" criterion)
- Regulatory technical standards on the conditions for assessing the materiality of extensions and changes of internal approaches for credit, market and operational risk (treatment of model extensions and model changes under the model review process)

All these EBA activities ultimately serve to harmonise the European rules, to ensure more consistent application of these rules and thus to directly reduce the supervisor-driven variability in model estimates.

Benchmarking in accordance with Article 78 of CRD IV: the EBA benchmarking exercise seeks to compare the estimates delivered by banks' models with each other. Benchmarking is the second key quantitative validation tool of internal models alongside backtesting (comparison of parameter prediction and parameter realisation within a bank). Benchmarking analyses the differences in model results that also occur if the internal models of different banks are applied to identical – hypothetical – portfolios and, under the IRB approach, also to individual exposures. Such differences frequently do not mean that model estimates are distorted. The fact that the methodology is based on hypothetical and not actual portfolios is also a reason to analyse the results with a certain amount of caution. National implementation of Article 78 of CRD IV in the German Solvency Regulation (*Solvabilitätsverordnung*) contains some guidance on this point (Section 6 (4) of the Solvency Regulation): where the comparison of model estimates reveals that risks have been underestimated, BaFin is required to take appropriate corrective measures. When doing so, it must ensure that these measures do not lead to any standardisation or preferred methodologies, do not create any false incentives and do not trigger any "herding" behaviour. Ultimately, however, the exercise creates a certain incentive to behave more in line with the market in regard to model estimates wherever this is not inconsistent with backtesting and, for example, to avoid aggressive parametrisation of the level of risk (calibration), which could underestimate risks. This exercise thus also helps reduce the variability in model results.

TRIM exercise 2017–2019: this is probably the biggest and most comprehensive effort worldwide at present to review internal models in the IRB approach (credit risk), IMA (market risk) and IMM (counterparty risk) areas. It is being performed by the European Central Bank and covers the big eurozone banks directly supervised by the ECB. These banks are the main users of internal models for the purpose of calculating Pillar 1 capital requirements. The TRIM exercise builds on the EBA requirements and exercises outlined above and fleshes these out where required. In its capacity as the competent authority, the ECB decides on the available options. The ECB also has discretionary power of its own in some cases. That is the case, for example, when it comes to setting the materiality threshold (1%–2.5%) where a default event is determined using the "90 days past due" criterion. The exact definition of default events is the key factor and the main starting point for harmonising the definition of default and thus also for estimating the prudential parameters PD, LGD and exposure at default (EAD). The results of the benchmarking exercises are also included in reviewers' analyses. Even if the ECB overshoots the mark here at times and oversteps its powers in some cases, these efforts will lead to a significant reduction of supervisor-driven model variability.

The results in all three aforementioned areas will be available by the end of 2020. They will significantly reduce model variability wherever appropriate. Fully eliminating variability is neither feasible nor sensible, however, for example, with existing differences in lending processes (see above) in mind. But an output floor is thus actually superfluous and the other approaches to reducing undue model variability are superior and more more effective.

7 European implementation of finalisation of Basel III (Basel IV)

The 2008 financial crisis highlighted the global danger of contagion in the financial markets and potential adverse consequences resulting therefrom. It thus demonstrated that uniform regulation of all major financial markets ultimately benefits all market participants, as financial crises cannot be confined to specific economic areas. The Basel capital framework is therefore a valuable asset that needs to be protected by ensuring that it is complied with. The new Basel framework should consequently also be implemented in Europe. That goes naturally on condition that all other members of the Basel Committee duly implement the framework as well, since essentially differing regulation causes serious distortions of competition that simply cannot be accepted for globally active financial institutions.

A key element of the new framework is the output floor for all standardised approaches. The necessity and sense of such a prudential tool sparked a highly contentious debate. The floor was introduced with the intention of effectively limiting, in a simple manner, variability in the results delivered by internal models. While this effect is undoubtedly achieved by the floor, it comes at a high price. This is because the floor actually prevents risk-sensitive capital backing, as the risk-sensitive measurement results delivered by models are ultimately adequately reflected only for poorer risks.

The problems posed by the output floor become obvious particularly in interaction with the standardised approaches (e.g., the credit risk standardised approach [CRSA]). In this context, the CRSA reform does indeed point in the right direction of a partial enhancement of risk sensitivity (e.g., through a refined sub-asset class structure). We therefore do not share the view that retaining the old CRSA would have an equivalent effect in prudential terms. Nevertheless, the CRSA – in the eyes of IRB model users, at any rate – is still not risk sensitive enough. This can be made clear if, for example, the CRSA is compared with the new sensitivity-based market risk standardised approach, which is much closer to an internal model-based approach than is the CRSA. There are also still too many exposures where the borrower's credit quality plays no part in risk weighting ("flat RWAs"). Furthermore, compared with the IRB approach, certain types of collateral are not recognised in the CRSA.

False prudential incentives to use an insufficiently risk-sensitive standardised approach are created in connection with application of the output floor: the capital requirements calculated on the basis of standardised approaches react less strongly or not at all to a change in the risk of a position. Under the IRB approach, for example, ratings have to be adjusted whenever the institution has new information on a borrower. As institutions have built up adequate data histories that also cover a financial crisis, internal rating procedures should be particularly well able to capture their risks accurately. When the floor comes into play, that is, the risk estimates delivered by an internal model are well below the floor level, the institution could increase risk under the risk measurement performed by its model without the standardised approach necessarily indicating higher risks (e.g., in the case of "flat RWAs"). This would have no impact on capital requirements until the floor level is reached. This effect is produced particularly by the typical risk overstatement under the standardised approaches in conjunction with the much too high floor of 72.5%.

Example: take a portfolio where the average IRB risk weight is 30% and the risk weight under the CRSA is 100% regardless of the amount of risk. The floor comes into play and is equivalent to a resulting risk weight of 72.5%. If the bank now increases the portfolio's credit risk, for example, by altering its lending behaviour, to 70% on average, this has no impact on capital requirements.

Europe did not need this floor, in our view. For one thing, there are the various sensible initiatives by European regulators and supervisors to curb internal model variability (see above) that will unfold their effect in the coming years. For another, the leverage ratio constitutes a risk-insensitive floor and therefore does not need to be backed by a further floor.

This, therefore, now raises the question of how Europe should design implementation of Basel IV. Firstly, European banks are likely to require a significant additional amount of regulatory capital. Secondly, the effect of risk-sensitive prudential tools adapted to the European credit markets will be restricted although, from a European perspective, this was unnecessary.

We take the view that, because of the need for global compliance, the output floor of 72.5% of the sum of RWAs calculated on the basis of standardised approaches should be introduced in Europe as well. After lengthy negotiations, Europe agreed to the introduction of this prudential tool and should consequently abide by the outcome of these negotiations. Despite this, we believe that ways of limiting the adverse effects of the floor need to be considered in European implementation.

As the floor achieves its effect through being linked to the standardised approaches, a reduction of its adverse effects could consist in complementing the current CRSA arrangements with a more risk-sensitive and better-calibrated standardised approach for a few selected portfolios. This could be designed as an option for institutions so that smaller institutions that have so far used the standardised approaches to calculate their regulatory capital are not forced to implement more complex, more risk-sensitive procedures.

Because of the European specificities, we believe that a more risk-sensitive CRSA option for at least two different asset classes is required: lending to unrated corporates and commercial real estate lending/specialised lending.

Elaborating concrete proposals is a task for the coming months. However, we should at this point already like to draw attention on two possible approaches:

Under the new CRSA, jurisdictions that do not allow any external ratings in the standardised approach may assign corporates that are identified as "investment grade" a preferential risk weight of 65%. This option should be additionally allowed in Europe as well. How classification as "investment grade" is to be determined – adapted to the European situation – still has to be clarified, however.

As far as specialised commercial real estate lending and other specialised lending are concerned, a risk-sensitive slotting approach could be developed for the CRSA, taking the current IRB slotting approach as its basis. The slotting approach for rating specialised lending is, as an IRB procedure, an already established – albeit little used – prudential tool. The four categories currently applying in Europe are inadequate, however. The number of categories could be increased to capture lower risks appropriately as well. At the same time, the classification criteria would need to be refined and fleshed out.

In conclusion, we should like to make a recommendation for a further important asset class. The CRSA sets out two approaches for determining residential real estate risk weights: the loan-splitting approach and the loan to value approach. Both should be eligible for use, depending on the structure of national real estate markets. Countries with a proven low loss history should at any rate be allowed to use the loan-splitting approach. Despite the trend towards minimising national options in Europe, the heterogeneity of the European real estate markets must be taken into account.

8 Summary

Given the deliberations on European implementation of Basel IV in CRR III starting in 2018, this article demonstrates that European – and especially German – banks are particularly affected. We expect the QIS, which we firmly support, to find that, contrary to the objective pursued by the European Council, capital requirements will increase significantly if the Basel rules are transposed into European law on an "as is" basis. This must be avoided. European banks are impacted in particular also because of their business and risk profile, reflected in, for example, the bank-based financial system, lending to SMEs largely without any external rating, and the national specificities of the European real estate markets, with traditionally low loss rates in, for example, Germany. On top of this, an output floor is actually unnecessary in Europe, since the European initiatives by the EBA and the ECB, presented above, sensibly address the problem of variability in model results by taking a cause-related approach and do not reduce the risk sensitivity of internal models simply and wrongly like the Basle Committee does through input and output floors. The Basel Committee has, in our view, taken the easy way out here. Nevertheless, for the sake of compliance with the Committee's compromise approach and to protect the future of international regulation, we do not call for not introducing the output floor in Europe. Instead, the problem of adverse floor effects we have outlined should be alleviated by at least making the CRSA more risk sensitive and, in particular, calibrating it better to good credit quality. We present initial proposals in this respect that can certainly be expanded upon in the further discussion.

Literature

Basel Committee on Banking Supervision 2017: Basel III: Finalising post-crisis reforms. (https://www.bis.org/bcbs/publ/d424.pdf)

Basel Committee on Banking Supervision 2017: Press release on "Basel III: Finalising post-crisis reforms". (https://www.bis.org/press/p171207.htm)

Association of German Banks 2014: Position paper of the Association of German Banks on retaining model-based capital charges. (https://bankenverband.de/media/files/BdB-PP_15072014-en.pdf)

European Banking Authority 2017: Ad Hoc Cumulative Impact Assessment of the Basel Reform Package. (https://www.eba.europa.eu/documents/10180/1720738/Ad+Hoc+Cumulative+Impact+Assessment+of+the+Basel+reform+package.pdf)

European Central Bank 2018<: Statistical Data Warehouse: Money, banking and investment funds. (http://sdw.ecb.europa.eu/reports.do?node=10000028)

Gaumert, Uwe 2013: Internals working? Regulators should keep internal models. In: RISK Magazine, August 2013, pp. 52–54. (https://www.risk.net/regulation/basel-committee/2282211/regulators-should-keep-internal-models)

Gaumert, Uwe/Kemmer, Michael 2015: Regulatory Developments in Risk Management: Restoring Confidence in Internal Models. In: K. Glau et al. (Ed.), Innovations in Quantitative Risk Management, Springer Proceedings in Mathematics & Statistics 99, Berlin, 2015, pp. 19–37. (https://link.springer.com/chapter/10.1007/978-3-319-09114-3_2)

Ossig, Christian 2015: Capital Markets Union: Process and priorities – A financial industry perspective. In: A. Dombret et al. (Ed.), The European Capital Markets Union – A viable concept and a real goal?, De Gruyter, Berlin, 2015, pp. 11–36

Ossig, Christian 2017: Banking sector diversity: Business finance and proportionate regulation. In: Journal of Money and Banking (Bancni vestnik), November 2017, pp. 42–47 (https://bankenverband.de/media/files/Gastbeitrag_CO_Slowenischer_Bankenverband.pdf

Shunsuke Shirakawa, Japan Financial Services Agency

Basel III – The view from Asia

General view on Basel III from Asian perspectives

The finalisation of Basel III is the final piece of post-crisis reforms (except for final review of the revised market risk framework) and expected to remove regulatory uncertainty. From the viewpoints of Asia which is located between the two major financial markets, the United States and Europe, the finalisation of Basel III is particularly welcomed because it would help maintain the multilateral framework of banking regulations and prevent fragmentation of global markets.

We respect the U.S. authorities who supported the Basel framework under the current U.S. administration advocating the policy of "America First." We also respect European authorities who finally accepted the compromise package despite diverse interests of European jurisdictions.

Japanese industry and general public showed at least lukewarm welcome to the agreement for the first time in the history of the Basel Committee. The extended negotiation period of last year, in my view, has caused Japanese banks' significant anxiety and, as an unintended but favorable consequence, made them fully aware of the importance of the multilateral regulatory framework underpinning their global activities.

In terms of overall impact of the finalisation of Basel III, capital requirements on Asian banks tend to be lessened because many of them use standardised approaches (or less advanced models) for risk-weighted asset (RWA) calculations and do not heavily rely on internal models, while actual impacts depend on how Basel III will be implemented in each jurisdiction.

On the other hand, major Japanese banks will face large increases in their capital requirements. They, however, appreciate the final adjustment made by the Basel Committee concerning constraints on the internal risk-based ("IRB") approaches to balance risk sensitivity with comparability and simplicity.

Note: Thank you very much for giving me an opportunity for representing Asia to express my views to so many distinguished experts.

https://doi.org/10.1515/9783110621495-017

Characteristics of Asian banks and implication of Basel III

Basel III has introduced additional constraints such as an aggregate output floor and input floors on IRB approaches in order to address excessive variability of RWA calculations. These measures may have different impact on each bank depending on its adopted business model. Asian banks, most of which are regarded as commercial banks, usually hold loan assets on their balance sheets until repayment and put more emphasis on internal credit assessment than investment banks. Thus, we need to carefully monitor whether these measures may unduly affect commercial banks vis-a-vis investment banks.

We need to carefully monitor how Basel III affects financial intermediation to small- and medium-sized enterprises ("SMEs"), which play important roles in Asian economies. The standardised approach on credit risk under Basel III has lowered risk weight for unrated SMEs from 100% to 85%, while there are other elements in Basel III such as the output floor that could have an adverse impact on SME financing.

Basel III may also affect trade finance, which supports Asian economies by facilitating international trade. Under Basel III, capital requirements for bank exposures will be increased by removal of both the advanced IRB approach and a certain standardised approach based on the creditworthiness of the sovereign of its jurisdiction of incorporation. Since trade finance usually relies on other banks' guarantee, these measures could in turn negatively affect trade finance in the Asian region.

In addition, Basel III may affect infrastructure financing, which is essential for sustainable growth of Asian economies. Since banks play important roles even in long-term financing in Asia, people are concerned about the impact of amendments to the treatment of specialised lending under Basel III.

There are other concerns as well. The new risk-sensitive framework of the standardised approach concerning real-estate financing (i.e., risk weight tables using loan-to-value ratios) would probably increase the overall capital requirement for those exposures, while they are expected to promote banks' robust risk management and to help prevent overheating of Asian property markets. In addition, the heightened risk weights for equity holdings (i.e., 250% risk weight) imply significant increase of capital requirements for Asian banks, especially for Japanese banks, while it is expected to help reduce cross-shareholdings with large corporates. Accordingly, these measures should be appropriate especially for Asian jurisdictions from a macro-prudential viewpoint.

What remains to be done

Though we have finalised the rule-making phase of Basel III, we are still facing significant challenges in its implementation phase. Since Basel rules concerning RWA calculations involve significant implications on level playing field concerns, it is all the more important for every jurisdiction to implement them in a globally harmonised manner. To be frank, Asian regulators are proud of our excellent track records in implementing Basel rules. Therefore, we would like to urge other major jurisdictions to implement Basel III faithfully in accordance with the agreed timeline.

In addition, it is important for us to evaluate effects of Basel III as well as its combined effects together with other post-crisis reform measures. The Japan Financial Services Agency has been claiming that we need to achieve not only financial stability but also economic growth by post-crisis reforms. In this respect, we are encouraged by the fact that both the Basel Committee and the Financial Stability Board have already embarked on impact assessment exercises and expect them to cover the areas I already mentioned. I believe we should not hesitate to make necessary adjustments if we find any unintended consequences.

Claudio Borio, Head of the Monetary and Economic Department, Bank for International Settlements

The geographical consequences of Basel III

After a long and at times painful process, we finally have an agreement. People say that the essence of a good compromise is that no one is happy. On that basis, this agreement must be a very good one! To be sure, all of us would have something to say and something to object to. For instance, as we heard at the conference from some distinguished academics, there are grounds for believing that the agreement may not be ambitious enough regarding minimum capitalisation levels. Indeed, an update of the BCBS (2010) long-term economic impact study done by colleagues of mine indicates that the room to further raise capital while providing net economic benefits was considerable, even on very conservative assumptions (Fender and Lewrick [2016]). But now we have it, and this was by no means assured a couple of months ago. The task is to implement the agreement in a full, timely and consistent manner.

We often hear that Basel III will have a large impact and constrain credit: according to this view, banks will have a hard time adjusting to it. In fact, I have a hard time understanding how this claim could be justified.

First, we should not forget that the latest data used to substantiate those claims relate to end-2015. In other words, they are stale, and banks have already had a couple of years of additional profits to make further progress. Moreover, there is a well-known Quantitative Impact Study (QIS) bias, which invariably leads to assessments that overestimate the degree to which the regulation is binding. And, make no mistake: banks will be "optimising" their portfolio and business decisions in the light of the new constraints: the final impact will be even smaller.

Second, it is common to hear that higher capital will constrain lending. And, yes, when the capital requirement is set as a ratio, banks may be tempted to respond to a higher one by adjusting their portfolio. Part of that adjustment could take the form of less lending. But this need not be the case. Indeed, credit has hardly been affected so far (Cohen and Scatigna [2014]). I do not expect things to be any different in the future, given how far the process has already gone. Moreover, we should not forget that capital is the basis for all lending, as common sense tells us and evidence confirms (e.g., Gambacorta and Shin [2017]). It is the best guarantee of *sustainable* lending – of banks' ability to support the economy through thick and thin. In the end, that is what really matters. "Fair weather" lending serves no one. The source of a credit crunch in some jurisdictions has more to do with the authorities' inability to clean up the balance sheets and recapitalise institutions than with anything else (Enria [2012], Borio [2016], Borio et al [2010]).

https://doi.org/10.1515/9783110621495-018

Finally, if some banks find it so hard to adjust to the latest requirements, they should raise profitability in the first place. Ultimately, it is profitability that holds the key to resilience. Granted, capital allows banks to absorb the immediate shock. But the recovery speed, and hence the costs to the economy, depend crucially on banks' earning capacity. Japan's experience following the burst of the credit bubble of the late 1980s is a sobering one. Seen through this light, the relatively low price-to-book ratios prevailing in some jurisdictions, not least in the euro area, are far from reassuring. The persistent and unusually low interest rates that have prevailed post-crisis have not helped, as the Japanese experience confirms. Raising profitability requires a multipronged approach: dealing aggressively with non-performing loans, where present; cutting costs, which have not declined much in several jurisdictions; and, above all, reducing excess capacity in the sector (Borio [2016]). Reducing excess capacity is essential in a number of jurisdictions (e.g., ESRB [2014]), and calls for policymakers' active support. I do not detect the necessary determination: for instance, in the euro area, policies are hardly supportive.

Let me also highlight a risk that is always around the corner: the risk of complacency. The risk is especially serious after such a wearisome policymaking process and when the economy is doing well. Thus, I could not agree more with Charles Goodhart, who made that very point during the conference. Indeed, if we factor in the discretionary phase-in period, Basel III will not be fully implemented until 2027: that is no less than some two decades following the outbreak of the crisis – 20 years! Financial cycles, whose peaks tend to coincide with banking strains, if not outright crises, tend to be as long or shorter (Borio [2014]). In my professional career, I have seen this complacency before. I saw it at the time of the Nordic crises, when those countries that had not yet gone through Norway's travails dismissed its experience as entirely idiosyncratic. And I saw again it in the run-up to the Great Financial Crisis, when western economies regarded the Japanese experience as an aberration. The refrain of the time from my supervisory colleagues still rings loud in my years as if it were today: "banks have never been as well capitalised as they are now ... their risk management has improved in leaps and bounds." We know how it all ended. We need to remain alert and not flinch when carrying the reforms through.

The questions I suggested to our panellists were as follows. What do you see as Basel III's main quantitative impact on the banks in your region? Do you see it as aligning mainly with regions, business models or even individual bank characteristics? Is Basel III the main constraint on your banks' behaviour or is it rather domestic regulatory and legislative initiatives? How do you expect banks to respond to Basel III in terms of their business models and types of activity? What is the outlook for "full, timely and consistent" implementation? How serious is the risk of regulatory fragmentation and, if it exists, is it because of stronger or weaker implementation in your region? This would make a world of difference: the former (stronger implementation) is consistent with the agreement's underlying philosophy – in this case, it would even be inappropriate to talk about "fragmentation" – the latter (weaker implementation) is not.

References

Basel Committee on Banking Supervision (BCBS) (2010): *An assessment of the long-term economic impact of stronger capital and liquidity requirements*, August.

Borio, C (2014): "The financial cycle and macroeconomics: what have we learnt?", *Journal of Banking & Finance*, vol 45, August, pp 182–98. Also available as *BIS Working Papers*, no 395, December 2012.

— (2016): "The banking industry: struggling to move on", keynote speech, Fifth EBA Research Workshop on "Competition in banking: implications for financial regulation and supervision", 28–29 November.

Borio, C, B Vale and G von Peter (2010): "Resolving the financial crisis: are we heeding the lessons from the Nordics?", *Moneda y Crédito*, no 230, pp 7–47. Also available as *BIS Working Papers*, no 311, July.

Cohen, B and M Scatigna (2014): "Banks and capital requirements: channels of adjustment", *BIS Working Papers*, no 443, March.

Enria, A (2012): "Supervisory policies and bank deleveraging: a European perspective", speech at the 21st Annual Hyman P Minsky Conference on the State of the US and World Economies, "Debt, deficits and financial instability", 11 April.

European Systemic Risk Board (ESRB) (2014): "Is Europe overbanked?", *Report of the Advisory Scientific Committee*, no 4, June.

Fender, I and U Lewrick (2016): "Adding it all up: the macroeconomic impact of Basel III and outstanding reform issues", *BIS Working Papers*, no 591, November.

Gambacorta, L and H S Shin (2017): "Why bank capital matters for monetary policy", *Journal of Financial Intermediation*, forthcoming. Also available as *BIS Working Papers* no 588, October 2016.

VII: Conclusion

Andrea Enria, Chairperson of the European Banking Authority

Basel III: "Are we done now? Not really"

Introduction

The reforms package agreed in December 2007 is a major achievement. The international regulatory community faced three key challenges. First, it was essential to remove regulatory uncertainty and bring the reform process to a close. The industry had rightly expressed serious concerns on the difficulty to perform effective capital planning in the absence of a complete regulatory framework, more than 10 years after the start of the financial crisis. Second, the credibility of international standards had to be restored, addressing the issue of excessive variability of risk-weighted assets (RWAs) calculated via internal models. To make this task more difficult, the Basel Committee had to strike a difficult balance between the need to maintain sufficient risk sensitivity, an important priority for jurisdictions widely relying on banks' internal models, and the quest to ensure a global level playing field, a significant concern for those jurisdictions that decided not to allow the use of model-based approaches. Third, it was necessary to reaffirm the commitment to the implementation of the full reform package in all G20 jurisdictions, resisting pressures to drop or significantly water down some key elements of the Basel Committee's rulebook. The crisis has damaged trust amongst regulators and convergence around stronger international standards was a key ingredient to restore the institutional setup supporting cross-border banking business. I believe the December agreement ticks all the three boxes.

I have repeatedly engaged for an agreement. At different stages of the debate, I flagged some concerns on the proposals being put forward by the Basel Committee. Since at least 2013, the European Banking Authority (EBA) has been monitoring the consistency of RWAs', acknowledging the need to address their excessive variability. We have actively promoted new rules and supervisory guidance to harmonise practices and re-establish the credibility of the framework. We supported the introduction of constraints to the use of internal models, especially in areas where they had a dismal track record. But we also warned against the risk of throwing away the baby with the bathwater, by significantly reducing the risk sensitivity of the framework. This is especially important to note, as the debate has been overly focused on the need to avoid a significant overall increase in capital requirements. To me, what mattered most was to prevent that the constraints to the use of internal models generated an inadequate redistribution of capital requirements, with unwarranted increases in the charges for low-risk business

https://doi.org/10.1515/9783110621495-019

and implicit incentives to shift towards riskier activities. I did not mind an increase in overall capital requirements, if there was a good, risk-based justification for it. Composition mattered more than level, in the matter at hand. The significant changes introduced following the public consultation allayed my concerns.

The core elements of the reform

In the area of *credit risk*, the agreed restrictions on the scope of loss-given default (LGD) estimation for low-default portfolios reflect evidence that LGD estimation and wholesale portfolios – as opposed to probability of default (PD) estimation and retail portfolios – are the most important targets when it comes to RWA variability within credit risk. In addition, the introduction of moderately calibrated input floors should help keep model risk and arbitrage practices at bay.

Operational risk is among the areas where – learning from the crisis and the recent empirical evidence – a regime shift was in my view most warranted, triggering a capital requirement increase, where needed. The Advanced Measurement Approach lent itself to far too opaque modelling choices and too heterogeneous model outcomes, in certain cases leading to undercapitalisation against the multiple and severe operational risk episodes that can materialise. The existence of several different standardised approaches did not promote comparability either. Against this backdrop, the replacement of all existing methods by the newly developed one, should substantially simplify the framework. However, maintaining risk sensitivity for operational risk is not an easy task. The rule design process has clearly shown this. It will be in my view essential to carefully test the newly proposed approach and, in particular, to understand the implications of the discretion that the Basel agreement introduces in relation to the historical loss component of the requirement – a choice that we will have to make at the EU level. It would be important to maintain some regulatory incentives for bank management to set in place internal mechanisms to effectively monitor and allocate capital for operational risk.

The decision to ban modelling for credit value adjustment (CVA) risk (*CVA-IMA*), in my view, is less straightforward, as it decreases risk sensitivity of capital requirements in this area. Back in 2015, the EBA warned legislators and other stakeholders about potential outcomes of excessive CVA risk, also in relation to the system of exemptions that apply in the EU, and started an ongoing monitoring of CVA risk. Our preferred route would have been to gradually eliminate those exemptions while re-calibrating the existing capital requirements framework.

As to the *aggregate output floor*, together with several other European members, the EBA expressed some scepticism, arguing that the leverage ratio represents a sufficient top-down constraint on the outliers of the RWAs calculation. Moreover, after extensive analysis of the problem of RWAs variability, our conclusion was that a bottom-up repair process, targeting specific areas where problems had been identified and focusing on harmonised definitions to enhance transparency and comparability, was preferable to a blunt output floor. In other words, to address the variability of modelling outcomes, we would have preferred to be digging at the roots instead of hacking at the leaves. However, we understand that this was an important component of the package for other authorities that rely mainly on the standardised approach. In light of the need to reconcile different views around the Basel table on the role of internal models in regulation, I believe that the final calibration of the output floor strikes a good balance.

The *standardised approach for credit risk*, which will drive most of the output floor constraining power, becomes a more risk-sensitive backstop. This is important not only because it makes the output floor backstop more responsive to risk, but also for the European population of smaller and less complex banks to which, in the EU, we traditionally extend the application of the Basel standards. There are several reasons to be satisfied about what the reform does in this area. While broadly remaining capital neutral, the reform of the standardised approach introduces enhanced risk differentiation and granularity in areas such as exposures secured by real estate, specialised lending exposures, exposures to small and medium enterprises (SMEs), unrated exposures to corporates and institutions, retail exposures, covered bond exposures as well as for equity exposures. In addition, in some of these areas, the new standardised approach moves closer to the European regulatory tradition.

There are aspects of the debate on the finalisation of Basel III on which we collectively will have to reflect. I firmly believe in the value of impact assessments to inform the choices of regulators and support an open public debate with all stakeholders on proposed reforms. Still, I am concerned when the whole debate is biased by an excessive focus on quantitative impact. We should remind ourselves that regulation aims at changing behaviour. Hence, quantitative impact assessments can provide useful input to discuss whether the behavioural effect will move in the right direction or could have unwarranted effects. Instead, the whole debate has been driven by a widely overestimated calculation of the capital impact from the industry, coupled with a rather simplistic syllogism equating higher requirements to lower lending and growth. The whole issue of ensuring that capital charges are correctly measuring risks and that variability across institutions remains within reasonable ranges never appeared in the discussions. Also from the regulators' side, excessive emphasis was put on the "no significant increase" objective. Some opaqueness in the Basel process, especially when the initial proposals started being revised without any public disclosure, has probably not helped supporting a better technical engagement with stakeholders.

Outstanding issues and way forward

One may be tempted to ask herself/himself the question: "Are we done now?" The short answer to that question is "not really." As for the longer answer, a few more considerations are probably needed.

Undoubtedly, the standards agreed by the Basel Committee now provide a good yardstick for long-term capital planning for international banks. Particularly in this case, I consider of the utmost importance that all G20 jurisdictions ensure a scrupulous adherence to the Basel Committee's rules text, at least for banks directly competing in international banking markets.

But any rule-making exercise is inevitably followed by an equally important and equally challenging implementation effort. From a European perspective, the way forward is threefold. In the first place, thorough analyses will be needed to ensure the international standards are transposed in accordance with the principle of proportionality, taking into account the compliance burden for smaller and less sophisticated local banks and considering the appropriateness of the impact on specialised business models. Secondly, we will need to complement the newly agreed framework with two equally important toolkits to address and monitor undue variability and potential arbitrage in the RWAs calculation. I am referring to, respectively, the bottom-up repair of modelling practices and the benchmarking analysis of internal models. Lastly, we will need to make sure enhanced transparency vis-à-vis the markets accompany the implementation of the newly agreed rules.

Proportionality in the implementation: the example of the Fundamental Review of the Trading Book

As regards the implementation of the standards, in the EU we have traditionally extended the Basel framework to all our institutions, not only to the larger and more internationally active ones, introducing deviations only where justified by sound empirical evidence. The Single Rulebook, built on the basis of this approach towards international standards, provided the EU financial system with an unprecedented set of harmonised rules as well as an essential condition of level playing field among players. The principle should not change this time: a rigorous and empirically grounded implementation strategy will be the key determinant of a successful reform.

As for past components of the Basel reform package, the EBA will conduct its assessment covering the implications of international standards on small and medium-sized banks, banks with simple or specialised business models as well as on lending to the real economy and to small and medium-sized enterprises.

Let me elaborate on the work we have done and are currently doing on the Fundamental Review of the Trading Book (FRTB), as this is a chapter on Basel framework that has recently attracted a good deal of discussion, and is a component on which our thinking is quite advanced.

Back in November 2016, recognising the compliance burden that certain elements of the new standards may imply for small and less complex trading book businesses, we have advised the Commission on a system of proportionality thresholds, whereby institutions with the smallest trading books may derogate market risk requirements and apply instead the credit risk framework, while institutions with a mid-tier trading book may keep applying a potentially recalibrated version of the current standardised approach for market risk (the Basel 2.5 approach), instead of the standardised approach reformed by the FRTB. The Commission has taken onboard this approach in the formulation of its legislative proposal. Last December, we launched a public discussion on technical although very relevant implementation aspects of the FRTB, among which the composition of the Profit and Loss (P&L) was used for the P&L attribution tests and the methodology to compute capital requirements on non-modellable risk factors.

As the Basel Committee decided to align the implementation of the FRTB to the timeline of the December 2017 package, acknowledging the need to further reflect on the technical implementation as well as the relative calibration, I have encouraged my staff to share with our Basel colleagues the technical options we have developed in the context of the EBA's work, as well as the evidence we are gathering around our proposals, not only on implementation issues, but also on relative calibrations and proportionality. Overall, there is merit in fine-tuning the relative distance between the newly introduced approaches – so as to target the initially envisaged modelling premium – while maintaining a less sophisticated standardised alternative. Such alternative could be the already existing (Basel 2.5) methodology, recalibrated to achieve levels of capital charge comparable with the ones of the new approaches.

Impact assessment analysis will have to cover other important chapters of the December 2017 package. Certainly, it will be crucial, from my perspective, to understand the risk-sensitivity implications of exercising the national discretion that the framework allows on the historical loss component of the operational risk requirement, particularly in light of the wide range of business models that characterises the EU banking market. In addition, we will have to look into aspects of implementation of the aggregate output floor and assess its impact on specialised business models, with particular focus on those that carry out their activities on the lower-tail of the risk distribution.

Regulatory bottom-up repair of internal models and benchmarking analysis

The second element of the agenda on the way forward is the bottom-up repair of modelling practices. As opposed to portfolio risk-driven variability, practice-based variability should be the target of supervisory action. Back in 2015, the EBA launched a public discussion – and subsequently a roadmap – on the repair of Internal Ratings-Based modelling. This led us not only to take stock of a very wide range of modelling practices – against which we proposed harmonised solutions – but also to fill the gaps that arise when regulatory provisions are not sufficiently clear or detailed.

The good news is that the project is almost accomplished. With the publication of the guidelines on the estimation of PD and LGD parameters, last November, the estimation of loss-given-default in conditions of economic downturn remains the last item to be accomplished. As per our tradition, the findings of our stock-take exercises are public: the guidelines on the parameters estimation have been accompanied by a report on IRB modelling practices that illustrates the great level of detail according to which 102 institutions from 22 Member States have been surveyed in relation to their modelling practices. We gave European institutions time to prepare for the application of the harmonised toolkit and we look forward to seeing that framework fully operational under the newly agreed credit risk standards.

The second complementary toolkit in the agenda is the benchmarking analysis. In order to monitor on an ongoing basis the variability of RWAs, and in order to identify those institutions that are true outliers, we will need to develop at the global level a systematic and consistent benchmarking framework. While the reform was being designed, much discussion on undue RWA variability focussed on either the relative distance between internally modelled and standardised requirement, which is the backbone of the output floor proposal, or on the simple distribution of aggregate RWA densities. The former approach assumes that standardised metrics may represent an absolute measure of risk, disregarding that within each of the regulatory buckets the actual performance of local portfolios or local business models may be very heterogeneous. The mere aggregate

RWA density metric does not offer any reference point and is notoriously driven by the joint action of portfolio risk, modelling practices and supervisory/regulatory segmentation.

In this context, benchmarking analysis offers a more comprehensive set of analytical possibilities and allows to take an "identify and investigate" type of approach, which is necessary to understand the true drivers of identified outlier positions. On the basis of the EBA experience, two dimensions along which the benchmarking analysis supplements the monitoring of RWA densities are worth mentioning. First, for the so-called low default portfolios, due to their wholesale nature, it was possible to ask banks to measure RWAs on sets of common obligors. In broad terms, this means looking at RWA distributions by controlling portfolio risk. Second, for the so-called high default portfolios – which are retail and hence more local in nature – a back-testing approach was taken, comparing model estimates with realised risk. Going forward, benchmarking may also be used to test the performance and convergence of specific sub-components of the IRB regulatory toolkit, which go beyond the PD, LGD or RWA estimation outcomes.

The EBA has an established benchmarking tradition that is enshrined in the law and, each year, is carried out through the publication of dedicated binding standards. EBA's experience is already shared with colleagues from other jurisdictions within technical groups of the Basel Committee. I encourage the Basel Committee to attach high priority to this type of work in its future agenda.

Transparency

Disclosure is certainly another of the priorities as the EU moves into the implementation phase. The compound set of regulatory changes that will become applicable in 2022 require both banks and supervisors to revisit the way risk is represented, both in terms of reporting requirements and requirements of disclosure towards the markets. At the EBA, work on these aspects is ongoing; the aim is to be able to implement these changes in a smooth and timely manner, so as to facilitate the implementation of the new rules. With the completion of the rule design phase, one of the duties we have vis-à-vis investors is to make sure the enhanced risk capture of the framework becomes fully accessible to them. Market discipline, exercised via Pillar III disclosure, is a component of the Basel regime that we cannot and should not undermine, in any way or form. The reform package includes transitional provisions and national discretions, on several fronts. I believe that, irrespective of the transitional path and of national choices on the optional components, disclosure should cover the fully fledged Basel framework. We not only have to put investors in a position to exercise their due diligence, but also we should avoid that incomplete disclosure translates into reputational problems and investors' decreased trust.

Conclusions

International standards are a common good for regulators and industry alike. When they lose credibility, it is not only the reputation of regulators that suffers: In the absence of reliable metrics, funding markets may enter into a freeze, with good and bad banks suffering alike. This has happened when the flaws of the regulatory definition of capital were exposed at the beginning of the crisis, as innovative instruments failed to provide the expected loss absorbency and continued paying coupons while governments were forced to put in place hefty public support packages. Similarly, as banks perceived to have similar portfolios started posting significantly different RWAs and bank managers started talking of "risk weight optimisation", public confidence in the reliability of internal models was damaged. The Basel Committee has now delivered on both fronts, putting the regulatory framework supporting international banking on a much stronger footing.

The ball is now in the court of the authorities in charge of implementing the last chapter of the reform. In the EU, the forthcoming renewal of the European Parliament and Commission in 2019 makes the timeline particularly challenging, due to the pause in legislative activity. The EBA stands ready to assist and conduct the preparatory technical work as soon as possible, with a view to ensuring a timely application of the international standards in 2022.

Bei Fragen zur Produktsicherheit wenden Sie sich bitte an:
If you have any questions regarding product safety,
please contact:

Walter de Gruyter GmbH
Genthiner Straße 13
10785 Berlin
productsafety@degruyterbrill.com